ESSENTIAL
LINK MODULES
Leaving Certificate Vocational Programme

Des Cusack

Published by
CJ Fallon
Ground Floor – Block B
Liffey Valley Office Campus
Dublin 22
www.cjfallon.ie

© Des Cusack

First Edition March 2010
This Reprint October 2010

Design and Layout Design Image

Acknowledgements
The author would like to thank all at CJ Fallon and his colleagues at the Salesian Secondary School, Limerick.

Dedication: To Margaret, Shane and Aisling, and my parents Mary and Ted.

Printed in Ireland by
Turner Print Group
Earl Street
Longford

Contents

Introduction

What is the LCVP?

The Leaving Certificate Vocational Programme (LCVP) – the 'enhanced Leaving Certificate' – is a two-year programme where students take **two Link Modules** as part of the Leaving Certificate. These Link Modules are:

* Preparation for the World of Work (Units 1–4); and
* Enterprise Education (Units 5–8).

Requirements for Participation in the LCVP

The requirements for participation in the LCVP are as follows:

* Students must take at least **five** Leaving Certificate subjects, including Irish.
* Two of these subjects must be from the designated Vocational Subject Groupings (published annually by the Department of Education & Science).
* Students must study the **two** Link Modules.
* Students must study a Leaving Certificate Modern European Language or an *ab-initio* course in a Modern European Language or a Vocational Language Module.

The LCVP was designed to enhance the vocational dimension of the Leaving Certificate. It combines the academic strengths of the Leaving Certificate with a focus on self-directed student-centred learning, comprising enterprise, work and the community.

Attention must be paid each year to the guidelines issued by the State Examinations Commission regarding the LCVP portfolio and examination, as changes do occur.

Assessment of the LCVP

At the end of the second year of the programme, as part of the Leaving Certificate, LCVP students must:

* Submit a **portfolio** comprising six items (worth 60% of the marks).
* Undertake a 2.5-hour **written examination** (worth 40% of the marks). The examination is based on the syllabus outcomes and activities covered in this book.

Assessment

60%

Portfolio
Core (Compulsory)
* Curriculum vitae.
* Summary report.
* Career investigation.
* Enterprise/action plan.

Optional (any two)
* Diary.
* Formal report.
* My own place report.
* Recorded interview/presentation.

40%

Written Examination
Section A
Audio visual questions (30 marks).

Section B
Case study questions (30 marks).
(Case study sent to schools in advance)

Section C
General questions: answer 4 out of 6 questions (100 marks).

For more detailed information, see the LCVP Portfolio Guidelines on page 122.

LCVP Accreditation

In the Leaving Certificate, the **Link Modules** are awarded and recognised as follows:

Grade	%	'Points'
Distinction	80–100	70
Merit	65–79	50
Pass	50–64	30
Fail	0–49	0

The results will appear on the normal Leaving Certificate results sheet.

 Remember: The portfolio alone is worth 60%.

LCVP Activities and Learning

In this book I have taken the eight units contained in the LCVP syllabus (four units in each Link Module) and given some background information and guidance. The book is a mixture of a textbook and a workbook. However, the emphasis must be on student-centred learning, where the student learns by doing. He/she engages in the activities and learns from their successes and/or failures.

Every LCVP activity should follow the basic steps (**P.E.E.R.**) outlined on the diagram on pages vii and viii.

As a student undertakes different LCVP activities, it is also important that he/she make use of other subject areas that he/she is studying. For example:
* **Business** is a relevant subject with regards to different types of businesses, enterprise skills and characteristics, report writing, industrial relations etc.
* **Geography** is important with regards to understanding the types of enterprises relevant to the area, reasons to locate in the area, 'My Own Place' report etc.
* Other subjects, such as **English**, **Irish** (e.g. place names), **History**, **Home Economics** and **Construction Studies**, are all very relevant to LCVP research and activities, especially enterprise activities, and the preparation of the LCVP portfolio items.

In this book, I am giving you the information to go out and complete the activities. The temptation to copy from a textbook, website, fellow student etc, must be avoided at all costs as it will be **heavily penalised** in the assessment.

P.E.E.R.: PREPARE ➡ EXPERIENCE ➡ EVALUATE ➡ RECORD

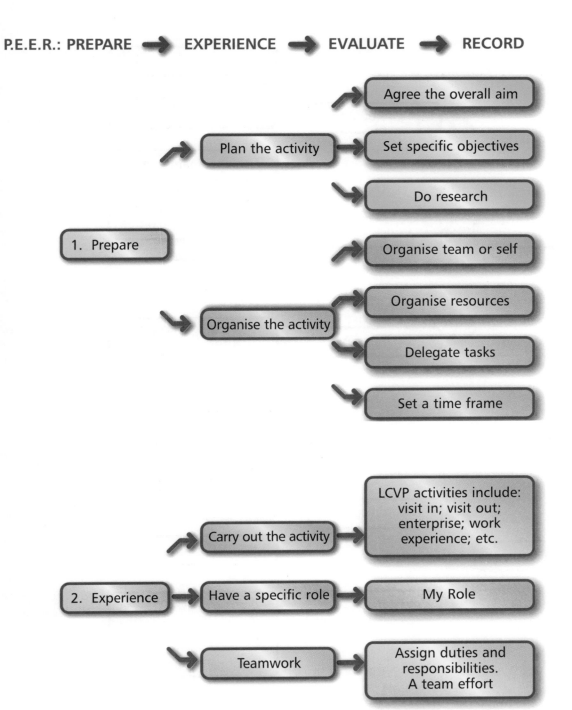

Agree the overall aim

Plan the activity → Set specific objectives

Do research

1. Prepare

Organise team or self

Organise resources

Organise the activity → Delegate tasks

Set a time frame

Carry out the activity → LCVP activities include: visit in; visit out; enterprise; work experience; etc.

2. Experience → Have a specific role → My Role

Teamwork → Assign duties and responsibilities. A team effort

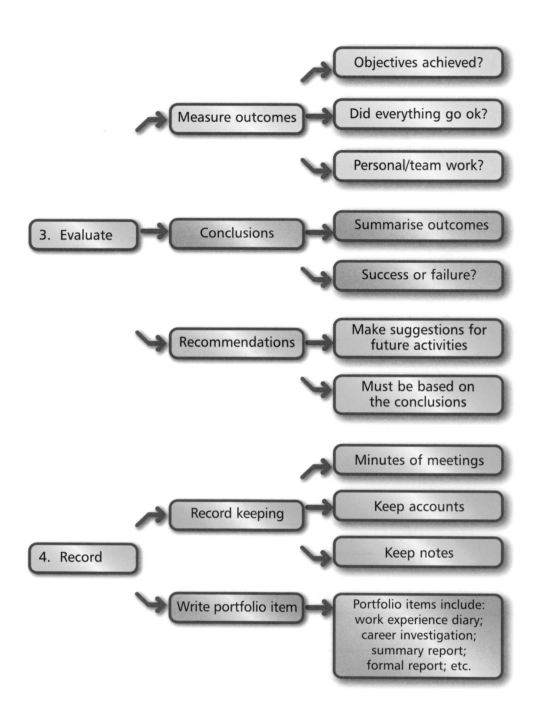

There are a range of tasks throughout the eight units that will help you to prepare portfolio items, as well as to prepare for the written examination. A separate section on 'Portfolio Guidelines' outlines clearly what you are expected to produce, with a suggested layout. There is also a section – 'My Portfolio' – where a blank template of each portfolio item is available, which you can complete prior to preparing the finished word processed documents.

Finally, the examination papers for 2005–2009 are included in this book so that all students can become familiar with the layout of the paper and the types of questions that are likely to appear in the examination.

Benefits of the LCVP

By undertaking the LCVP, students are encouraged to do the following.
* Be innovative and enterprising.
* Take responsibility for their own learning.
* Adapt to changing circumstances.
* Evaluate data and devise solutions to problems.
* Communicate their thoughts and ideas effectively.
* Work with others as part of a team.
* Investigate and plan career options.
* Use information and communication technologies.
* Investigate local business and community enterprises.
* Learn from their experiences.
(Source: Leaving Certificate Vocational Programme [syllabus]).

The student will also benefit in a variety of other ways, including the following.
* Having an enhanced curriculum vitae (CV) because of the additional activities undertaken.
* Benefit from the 'points' in their Leaving Certificate.
* Partake in work experience and possibly obtain a reference.
* Get recognition (and points) for activities that all Leaving Certificate students undertake regardless, e.g. CV, investigating career options etc.
* Be better prepared for interviews and/or presentations, and have more activities and experiences to talk about.

I hope that you enjoy participating in the LCVP and that this book is a useful tool in completing the activities, the portfolio and the examination successfully.

Des Cusack

LINK MODULE 1

PREPARATION FOR THE WORLD OF WORK

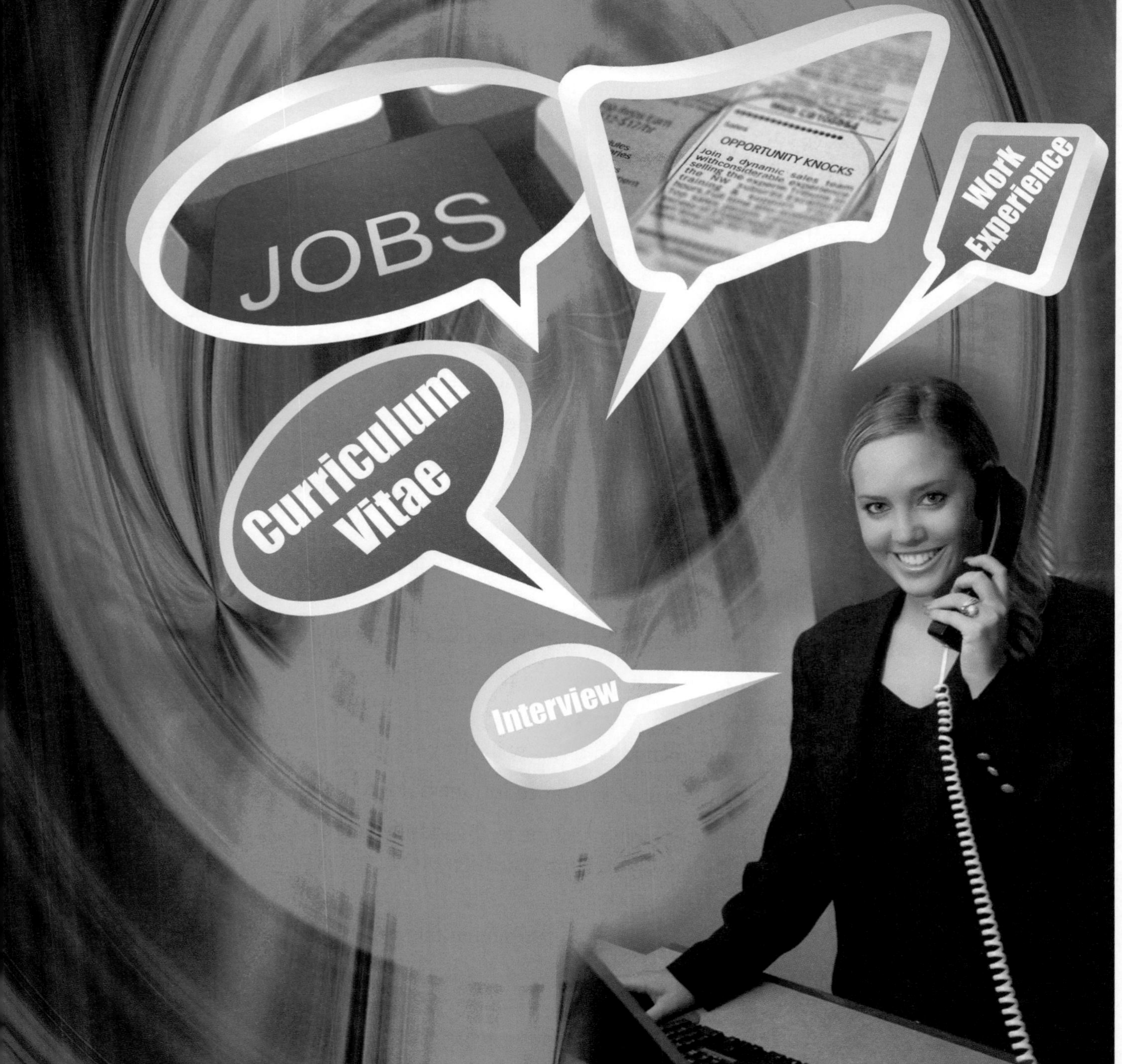

1

Introduction To Working Life

At the end of this chapter students should be able to (tick ✓ the box when completed):

* Identify the main sources of employment in the local area. ☐

* Identify the main social services and job creation agencies in the local area. ☐

* Identify the main agencies that provide transport in the local area. ☐

* Identify the main financial institutions servicing the needs of the local area. ☐

* Identify the main agencies involved in industrial relations in the local area. ☐

* Identify the principal economic activities in the local area. ☐

* Evaluate the potential for tourism in the local area. ☐

* Identify and understand the main differences between school and work. ☐

* Describe the intrinsic value of various forms of work including self-employment and voluntary work. ☐

* Understand current regulations/legislation relating to the employment of young workers. ☐

* Understand current health and safety regulations in workplaces. ☐

* Role-play a situation that could give rise to a dispute in the workplace. ☐

* Understand issues related to diversity in the workplace. ☐

* List the different forms of assistance for unemployed people. ☐

* Arrange a visit to a training scheme in the locality and/or invite an appropriate speaker from such an organisation to visit the group in the school. ☐

* Link the activities in this unit to learning in relevant Leaving Certificate subjects. ☐

Part 1 | Workplace

Work vs Employment

Work is defined as any activity or task for which we are **not** paid. On the other hand, employment is when we work and get paid for it. For example, when a hairdresser cuts the grass at home that is described as work, whereas when the hairdresser cuts a client's hair that is described as employment.

Work: 'not paid'.
Employment: 'paid'.

Differences between School and Employment (Paid Work)

Some the main differences between going to school and going to work (i.e. employment) include:

Pay vs no pay

School uniform vs no uniform

Moving out from home

Have responsibilities and can be fired

Differences

Money management

Employee legislation

Training/qualifications

Contract of employment

Task

Discuss these differences between school and employment in the classroom. Explain any five differences.

1. _____

_____

2. _____

_____

3. _____

_____

4. _____

_____

5. _____

_____

Can you think of any other differences between going to school and being in employment?

1. _____

2. _____

Value of Work

When you go to work, you may be working for somebody else (you are an employee) or you may be self-employed. Either way, there are a lot of benefits to be gained, both financial and non-financial, including the following.

	Financial Benefits	Non-Financial Benefits
Employee	✳ Wages/salary. ✳ Bonus. ✳ Benefit-in-kind, e.g. car. ✳ Overtime.	✳ Security: able to plan for the future. ✳ Self-esteem: being useful, doing worthwhile things. ✳ Promotion: good for morale and motivation. ✳ Possibility of travel. ✳ Acquire new skills/ experiences/qualifications. ✳ Acquire new friends: social aspect.
Self-employed	✳ Wages/salary. ✳ Benefit-in-kind, e.g. car. ✳ Share of profit/dividends.	✳ Being your own boss/make decisions. ✳ Self-esteem: doing something worthwhile. ✳ Sense of achievement. ✳ Respect. ✳ Possibility of travel. ✳ Acquire new skills/experiences. ✳ Security: able to plan for the future.

It is also possible that you might be engaged in **voluntary work**, e.g. for a charity or local organisation, or some other unpaid work at home or abroad. This is particularly useful at a time of recession when you might otherwise be unemployed. There are also a lot of benefits to be gained from this type of work including the following.

✳ Helping others.
✳ Acquiring new skills and experiences.
✳ Improved curriculum vitae – new skills/experiences.
✳ Enhanced reputation and respect.
✳ Sense of achievement.
✳ Achieving one's own goals, i.e. self-actualisation.
✳ Possibility of employment, should a vacancy arise.

Task

Name a voluntary organisation in your local area. _____

What possible skills or experience could you gain as a volunteer working for this organisation? _____

_____

_____

_____

Can you name any organisation that looks for volunteers to work abroad?

_____

Employment of Young Workers

An important piece of legislation protecting young workers under the age of 18 years is the **Protection of Young Persons (Employment) Act, 1996**.

Under 18 year olds Protection of Young Persons (Employment) Act, 1996

Maximum Hours of Work Per Week

Under 18s may not be employed for more than 40 hours a week or 8 hours a day, except in a genuine emergency. The maximum weekly hours for 14 and 15 year olds are:

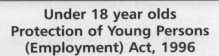

Age	14	15
Term-time	Nil	8 hours
Holiday work	35 hours	35 hours
Work experience	40 hours	40 hours

Age Limits

For a regular job, the general minimum age is 16. Employers can take on 14 and 15 year olds for light work:

- Part-time during the school term (over 15 only).
- As part of an approved work experience or educational programme.
- During the school holidays, provided there is a minimum three week break from work.

Early Morning and Night Work

The hours permitted are:

Age	Under 16s	16 and 17s
Early morning	After 8am	After 6am
Night work:		
– school next morning	Up to 8pm	Up to 10pm
– no school next morning	Up to 8pm	Up to 11pm (7am next morning)

Rest Breaks

Age	Under 16s	16 and 17s
30 min break	4 hours	4.5 hours
Every 24 hours	14 hours off	12 hours off
Every 7 days	2 days off	2 days off

Exceptions and Penalties

The full provisions of the Act do not apply to:

- Employment of close relatives.
- Employment in fishing, shipping or defence forces.

Offenders could face fines up to €1,904.61, and an extra €317.43 a day for a continuing offence.

Notes

1. This extract from the Act is taken from a poster provided by the Department of Enterprise, Trade and Employment, and is not meant to be a legal interpretation. Further information can be obtained from: www.entemp.ie.
2. This Act also outlines the **Duties of Employers** who employ young workers, including:
   * They must see a copy of the birth certificate and, before employing someone under 16, must get the written permission of the parent or guardian.
   * They must keep a register containing the following particulars of each person employed under 18 years of age – full name, date of birth, time work starts, time work finishes, rate of wages/salary paid, total amount of wages/salary paid.
3. Complaints about breaches of the Act may be made in confidence to: Labour Inspectorate, Department of Enterprise, Trade and Employment, Davitt House, 65A Adelaide Road, Dublin 2. The Department's Inspectors have powers to go into places of work, question employers and employees, and examine records. Parents may refer certain breaches of the Act to a Rights Commissioner.

Young workers are also protected by a number of other Acts, including the following.

Safety, Health and Welfare at Work Act, 2005

Consolidates and updates existing safety and health legislation – see the Health & Safety section in this unit. It also imposes more serious penalties for breaches of the legislation.

Equality Act, 2004 (amended Employment Equality Act, 1998)

Prohibits discrimination for employment on nine grounds – gender, marital status, age, family status, race, religious belief, disability, sexual orientation, and member of the Traveller community. This Act also prohibits sexual harassment and other forms of harassment.

Protection of Employees (Part-Time Work) Act, 2001

This Act applies to any part-time employee working under a contract of employment or apprenticeship. The Act provides that a part-time employee cannot be treated in a less favourable manner than a comparable full-time employee in relation to the conditions of employment. All employee protection legislation applies to part-time employees.

National Minimum Wage Act, 2000

In 2009 the national minimum hourly rate of pay was €8.65.

Employee	Minimum hourly rate of pay	%
Experienced adult worker	€8.65 per hour	100
Under age 18	€6.06 per hour	70
First year from date of first employment over age 18	€6.92 per hour	80
Second year from date of first employment over age 18	€7.79 per hour	90

Source: www.citizensinformation.ie

Organisation of Working Time Act, 1997

A part-time employee's minimum annual leave entitlement is:

* Four working weeks in a leave year in which a part-time employee works at least 1,365 hours.
* One-third of a working week per calendar month that the part-time employee works at least 117 hours.
* 8% of the hours worked in a leave year subject to a maximum of 4 working weeks.

Note: Some employers add 8% holiday pay onto the pay rate so as to cover your entitlements under this Act.

Contract of Employment

All employees are entitled to receive a written contract of employment. This contract will include the following.

* Employer's name and address.
* Job title.
* Job description.
* Wages/salary.
* The procedure for dismissal.
* Hours to be worked.
* Holiday entitlements.
* Date of commencement.
* Deductions from wage/salary.
* Employee's name and address.

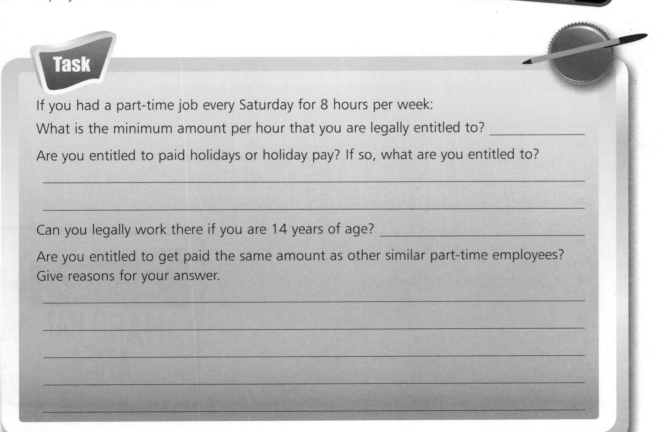

Task

If you had a part-time job every Saturday for 8 hours per week:

What is the minimum amount per hour that you are legally entitled to? _____

Are you entitled to paid holidays or holiday pay? If so, what are you entitled to?

_____

_____

Can you legally work there if you are 14 years of age? _____

Are you entitled to get paid the same amount as other similar part-time employees? Give reasons for your answer.

_____

_____

_____

_____

_____

FIRST AID STATION

Health and Safety Regulations

It is very important for every workplace to:
* Prevent accidents happening to employees, customers and the visiting public.
* Maintain hygiene standards.
* Protect the security of the workplace.
* Prevent bullying and harassment in the workplace.

To this end, **The Safety, Health and Welfare at Work Act, 1989,** as well as the **Safety, Health and Welfare at Work Regulations, 1993,** set out the legal requirements to safeguard workplaces. The Health & Safety Authority (HSA) is responsible for implementing, monitoring and investigating the provisions of the Act and their enforcement.

Statistics

In 2008, a total of 57 fatalities in the workplace were reported to the HSA. Of these:
* 15 deaths were in the construction industry.
* 21 deaths were in the agriculture/hunting/forestry industry.
* 6 deaths were in the manufacturing industry.

In 2009, there were a total of 41 fatalities in the workplace up to mid-December. Some 28,800 employees were absent 4+ days as a result of injury in the workplace in 2007.
Source: www.hsa.ie.

Every workplace is required to compile a 'Safety Statement' that identifies all the potential hazards, the risk involved, and the safety procedures and guidelines.

Employers must:
* Provide information, training and supervision when appropriate. This includes safety training courses, fire drills, warning notices, etc.
* Highlight and protect employees from potential hazards.
* Provide a safe working environment, e.g. machinery with safety features, restricted access.
* Provide safety equipment and clothing, and enforce their use.
* Record accidents and injuries, and take preventive action.
* Facilitate the appointment of a safety representative from the workforce.
* Investigate claims of bullying/harassment.
* Have an anti-bullying policy in place, with agreed procedures.

DANGER HARD HAT AREA

Employees also have their own responsibilities, including:
* Following safety instructions and procedures.
* Wearing safety clothing.
* Reporting injuries and hazards.
* Using machinery and equipment carefully and responsibly.
* Treating everybody with respect, e.g. do not bully others.

Since 2004, smoking in the workplace is banned for workers and members of the public. Additional information and updates can be obtained from the Health & Safety Authority website www.hsa.ie.

Task

In pairs, carry out a health and safety audit of your school, with each pair assigned to a different area or department. Be sure to get permission. (You could write a summary report on this activity – see summary report layout.)

Identify the main health and safety features. What, in your opinion, are the principal risks/hazards? What recommendations would you make to improve health and safety?

Diversity in the Workplace

A workplace can be made up of a variety of people of different sexes, ages, races, cultures, political beliefs, interests, hobbies, tastes etc. Such diversity can create issues in the workplace. The Equality Act 2004 amended and upgraded the Employment Equality Act 1998. These Acts deal with some of the issues that arise:

* Discrimination is outlawed on nine distinct grounds: gender, religious belief, marital status, family status, age, sexual orientation, race, disability, and membership of the Traveller community. Discrimination is when one person is treated in a less favourable way than another person is, or would be, treated. This applies to all full-time and part-time employees.
* Harassment is defined as any act or conduct which is unwelcome and offensive, humiliating or intimidating on a discriminatory ground including spoken words, gestures, or the production, display or circulation of written material or pictures. Harassment and sexual harassment are illegal under the Acts. It applies to the actions of employees, the employer, customers and business contacts.
* All employees are entitled to equal pay for like work.
* The Office of the Director of Equality Investigations was set up by the Act to investigate cases of discrimination (except dismissal and gender cases).
* The Equality Authority was established by the 1998 Act to promote equality of opportunity (www.equality.ie).

Task

Topics for Discussion

* **Sex stereotyping** – making assumptions that there is a distinction between "men's work" and "women's work", or distinguishing between men and women when it comes to career paths or roles. Do you agree or disagree? Give examples.

* **'Glass ceiling'** – there is a gender imbalance in the higher levels of management, and women find it particularly difficult to rise above a certain level. Do you agree?

* **Religion** – recognition of certain religious holidays and not others. Should all major religious holidays be recognised or should none be?

* **Dress codes** – should they allow for different tastes, cultural and religious differences in schools and/or the workplace?

* **Disabilities** – is your school or workplace accessible for people with disabilities? How does this affect their career opportunities?

Disputes in the Workplace

Disputes can occur for a variety of reasons, including the following.

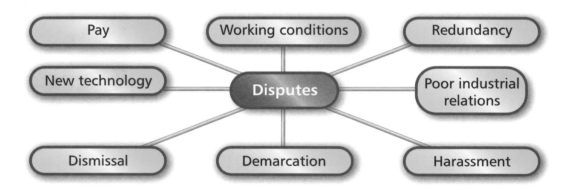

(Note: a demarcation dispute occurs over which employee is supposed to carry out a specific task, especially if it was not previously agreed.)

In dealing with a dispute, the worker may initially try to solve the problem on his or her own, e.g. by going to management. If this is unsuccessful, he/she may then approach the **shop steward** of the union in the workplace (assuming there is a trade union and he/she is a member). The shop steward is the trade union representative in the workplace. It is a voluntary unpaid role. The shop steward will represent the workers on trade union matters and communicate and negotiate with management.

Role of a Trade Union

* Protects workers' interests, and rights, in their dealings with the employer.
* Negotiates with employers so as to improve the pay and working conditions of their members.
* Represents the employees in disputes, and as a result have greater strength at the negotiating table.
* Will negotiate redundancy payments when there are possible job losses.
* May also negotiate discounts with service providers on behalf of members and provide additional services, e.g. discounts for health insurance, credit union membership etc.

If unsuccessful in resolving the dispute, the shop steward will then contact trade union headquarters and request the assistance of a trained full-time trade union official. This official will then visit the workplace and represent the worker(s) in attempting to solve the dispute.

If the dispute remains unresolved at this stage, both parties will most likely resort to the State's industrial relations mechanisms and institutions for resolving disputes. These include the following.

* The **Labour Relations Commission (LRC)** – offers an Industrial Relations Officer to provide a conciliation service. Conciliation involves listening to both sides and attempting to bring about negotiation and reconciliation (www.lrc.ie).
* The LRC also provides a **Rights Commissioner** to investigate disputes involving one worker or a small group. The Rights Commissioner deals with a wide range of legislation, including the Unfair Dismissals Acts, Protection of Employees Acts, Safety Health & Welfare at Work Act, Terms of Employment Act, and so on.
* The LRC also provides **advisory and mediation services**.
* **Equality Officers** who investigate formal complaints regarding discrimination. These are appointed by the Director of the Equality Tribunal. (Director of Equality Investigations.)
* **The Labour Court** – a court of final appeal. It investigates disputes and issues recommendations. It also hears appeals concerning Rights Commissioners and Equality Officers – it is only legally binding in these cases.

Websites
www.lrc.ie
www.labourcourt.ie
www.entemp.ie
www.basis.ie
www.whoisireland.com
www.business2000.ie
www.employmentrights.ie

Task

Using the Internet, research the following.

* A workplace dispute – what was it about and how was it resolved (www.google.ie).
* How many strikes occurred, and/or how many days were lost due to strikes, in Ireland for the most recent year on record (www.cso.ie).

Assistance for Unemployed People

There are a variety of payments available from the Department of Social and Family Affairs, and elsewhere, for people who are unemployed (or who work less than 3 days a week). These include the following:

* **Jobseeker's Benefit** – payable to those who have lost their jobs. It is a weekly payment based on your earnings and your PRSI contributions in the relevant tax year. It is payable for a maximum of 12 months. You must be available for work.

* **Jobseeker's Allowance** – a weekly payment to those not eligible for jobseeker's benefit, or when the benefit expires. It is means tested. In 2009 the maximum **personal** rate was €204.30 per week. (There are further payments available for applicants with a dependent adult and/or children.) The personal rate of jobseeker's allowance is €100 for new claimants under 20 years of age (2009).

* **Family Income Supplement (FIS)** – in order to qualify for FIS, the net average family income must be below a specified amount for the size of your family, e.g. for a family with three children it is €685 per week (2009). The FIS is worth 60% of the difference, subject to a minimum of €20 per week. Those eligible will also qualify for the 'back-to-school payment' and the 'smokeless fuel allowance'. Medical card eligibility is not affected.

* **Revenue Job Assist** – a tax allowance for people returning to work after being unemployed for at least 12 months. The tax allowance can be claimed for three years.

* **Back to Work Enterprise Allowance** – encourages unemployed people to return to work by setting up their own enterprises (become self-employed) by allowing them to retain a part of their social welfare payments for 2 years:
  * 100% of the social welfare payment in the 1st year.
  * 75% of the social welfare payment in the 2nd year.

* **Part-time Job Incentive Scheme** – this scheme allows people who have been receiving the jobseeker's allowance for at least 15 months to take up part-time work and still receive a part-time job allowance.

* **Back to Education Allowance** – this aims to encourage unemployed people to return to education and acquire extra qualifications or retraining. People who undertake such courses qualify for social welfare payments. To qualify for the second level option you must be receiving a qualifying social welfare payment for 3 months. You must also be a jobseeker and out of the formal education system for at least 2 years. To qualify for the third level option you must be receiving a qualifying social welfare payment for 9 months in line with the National Employment Action Plan.

Websites
www.welfare.ie
www.citizensinformation.ie
www.cso.ie
www.revenue.ie
www.hse.ie
www.education.ie

There are also a variety of organisations providing courses for the unemployed, or those who work part-time, such as training, retraining, information courses, starting up a business etc. These organisations include the following.

✳ **FÁS** – provides a range of services and courses for the unemployed and those seeking work for the first time (www.fas.ie). These include being able to place your curriculum vitae (CV) on their computer system and being paid while training. Their courses include:

   ● Training courses.
   ● Apprenticeships.
   ● Community employment programmes (provides people with an opportunity to engage in useful work within their community on a part-time or temporary basis and expand their experience and skills).
   ● Start your own Business/Enterprise.

✳ **Irish National Organisation of the Unemployed** – provides training courses on social welfare and employee's rights at work. They also have advice and information centres (www.inou.ie).

✳ **Local Development Social Inclusion Programme** (LDSIP) – part of the National Development Plan, and co-financed by the EU, the LDSIP targets disadvantaged individuals and communities including the long-term unemployed, the underemployed, young people at risk, refugees, disadvantaged communities, low-income farm households, the homeless, etc. Services for the unemployed include advice, guidance, training initiatives and development of self-employment initiatives.

✳ **LEADER Programme** – a scheme part-funded by the EU to help rural communities to develop their own areas according to their own priorities. Funding is provided for a variety of initiatives including training and recruitment projects. This organisation will have a key role to play in building small enterprise and services in rural areas.

✳ **Rural Social Scheme** – a scheme which allows low-income farmers and fishermen/women to earn extra income working in the local community. This scheme is funded by the Department of Community, Rural and Gaeltacht Affairs.

> By 2009 these various local organisations have been merged into 36 'LEADER-Partnerships' (Local Action Groups) to deliver both LEADER and social inclusion funding. Every part of rural Ireland has a LEADER company to which interested parties can apply for support, advice and limited grant aid.
> For a full list see
> www.teagasc.ie/ ruraldev/links/ leader_partnerships.asp

✸ **Area Partnership Companies** – these companies promote job creation and enterprise in designated disadvantaged urban areas. Examples include: Ballyfermot Partnership, Galway City Partnership, Waterford LEADER Partnership Ltd, West Limerick Resources Ltd, PAUL Partnership Limerick and County Cavan Partnership. Services include: training in enterprise and job skills, access to further education, and grants and a mentoring service (a mentor is an experienced individual who can offer advice and guidance on an on-going basis) for start-up businesses. This is supported by the Local Development Social Inclusion Programme.

Websites
www.limceb.ie
www.corkceb.ie
www.dceb.ie
www.wceb.ie
www.pobail.ie
www.startingabusinessinireland.com/dirapc.htm
www.planet.ie
www.teagasc.ie
www.paulpartnership.ie

Task

Write a paragraph describing the function and services of each of the following:
(a) FÁS.
(b) Enterprise Board.
(c) Area Partnership Company.

Part 2 | My Own Place

Throughout the LCVP syllabus there is a focus on the local area surrounding your school and home. The purpose behind this is to make students more aware of their own area, including employment opportunities, economic activities, financial institutions, voluntary groups, social services, agencies involved with enterprise/tourism/job creation etc. It also encourages the establishment of school and community links, e.g. visits in/out and work experience.

The first step in researching the local area is to define the local area, i.e. set boundaries.

Task

Where is your local area? How far does it extend? What is the size of the population approximately? Is the area urban or rural? What are the main features, e.g. port, railway etc?
(Suggestion: obtain a map or draw a map outlining your local area.)

Economic Activities

Economic activity describes the different types of businesses that exist to provide us with the goods and services that we want and need.

Economic activities can be divided into three categories: primary, secondary and tertiary.

Category	Economic Activity
Primary (the extractive industries)	✳ Farming, e.g. tillage, dairy cattle, sheep. ✳ Fishing: inland and sea fishing. ✳ Forestry. ✳ Mining, e.g. Bord na Mona, windfarms.

Secondary	✳ Construction.
	✳ Manufacturing.
	  ● Agribusiness (e.g. food-processing).
	  ● Transnationals (e.g. Intel).
	  ● Irish owned.

Tertiary (services)	✳ Retailers (i.e. shops) ✳ Wholesalers (e.g. cash and carry wholesaler). ✳ Financial institutions. ✳ Tourism services (e.g. hotels, B&Bs, camping). ✳ Transport (e.g. bus, taxi, courier, truck). ✳ Legal (e.g. solicitors). ✳ Public services (e.g. schools, clinics, libraries, parks).

Sources of Employment

When identifying the main sources of employment in your own area it is a good idea to divide the employment into different categories, e.g. the main economic activities.

Insert the name of at least one employer from your area in each of the following boxes:

Primary

Farming:

Fishing:

Forestry:

Mining:

Secondary

Construction:

Irish Manufacturer:

Agribusiness:

Transnational (multinational):

Tertiary

Retailer:

Bank:

Solicitor:

Transport:

Task

(a) Name two other service providers in your area.

(b) Identify the type of business organisation of **each** of the above employers. Are they sole traders, partnerships, limited companies, co-operatives etc? Is the business indigenous (Irish owned), a multinational or a franchise?
Ask your business teacher for assistance – you could use this research and information as part of a report (a portfolio item).

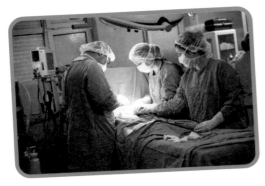

Services and Institutions in the Local Area

Identify examples of **each** of the following in your local area.

Social services

These include agencies such as hospitals, clinics, social welfare offices (Department of Social and Family Affairs), citizen advice centres, and voluntary organisations such as St Vincent De Paul.

Task

Identify the main **social services** in your area.

_____

_____

_____

_____

Job creation agencies

The main job creation agencies include Enterprise Boards, LEADER Partnerships, IDA Ireland, Shannon Development, Area Partnership Companies, FÁS, Obair, etc.

Task

Identify the main **job creation agencies** in your area.

_____

_____

_____

_____

Industrial relations

The term 'industrial relations' describes the relationship that exists between employers and employees in the workplace. There are a large number of organisations involved in either representing or lobbying on behalf of employers or employees, or organisations involved in promoting good industrial relations and helping to solve conflict.

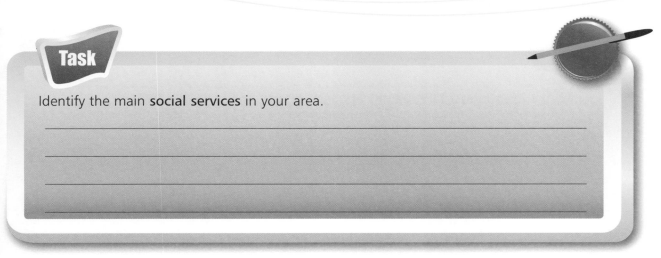

These organisations include:

* **Trade unions** – represent and negotiate on behalf of employees, e.g. SIPTU.
* **Irish Business and Employers Confederation (IBEC)** – represent employers and businesses.
* **Chambers of Commerce** – a local association of businesses and employers. Can act as a local mediator (conciliation) in the case of a dispute.
* **Management consultants** – offer advice to businesses for a fee.
* **Labour Relations Commission (LRC)** – provide a conciliation service for industrial disputes nationwide. Also carries out research and gives advice on industrial relations.
* **Labour Court** – this is not a court of law. It is the court of appeal for industrial relations matters. This is the final recourse to solve disputes.

Task

Identify the main **industrial relations agencies** in your area.

_____

_____

_____

Financial institutions

The main financial institutions servicing the needs of the local area include the following.

* The commercial banks (e.g. Allied Irish Bank, Bank of Ireland, National Irish Bank, Ulster Bank).
* The building societies (e.g. EBS, Irish Nationwide).
* Credit unions.
* Insurance companies (e.g. Irish Life, Hibernian Aviva, Quinn Insurance) or brokers.

Task

Name the main **financial institutions** in your area.

_____

_____

_____

Transport

The main agencies providing transport in a local area include bus companies, taxis, train services (passenger and/or freight), local airports, haulage companies and couriers.

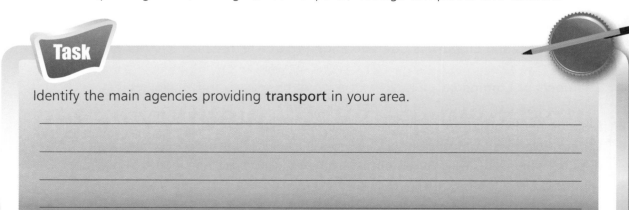

Task

Identify the main agencies providing **transport** in your area.

_____

_____

_____

Tourism

In examining the potential for tourism in an area, the following should be considered.

* Places of historical interest, e.g. castles.
* Scenery.
* Geographical features, e.g. lake, forest, beach.
* Recreational facilities, e.g. golf courses, swimming pool.
* Hotels and guesthouses.
* Shopping facilities.
* Restaurants.
* Night life, e.g. nightclubs, pubs, concerts.
* Transport.
* Heritage centre.
* Craft enterprises.

 Task

Highlight what you consider to be the main **tourist attractions** of your area (use the above list as a guideline).

_____   _____

_____   _____

_____   _____

_____   _____

 Task

(a) Take **one** aspect of your local area (e.g. tourist attractions) and write down a list of questions (questionnaire) that you could ask, or research, so as to obtain specific information about your chosen aspect.
Note: the LCVP class could be divided into groups and each group could be assigned a different aspect of the local area to investigate. The findings could then be amalgamated as part of the 'My Own Place' report.

(b) Are there any issues facing your local area, e.g. unemployment, lack of recreational facilities etc? Identify two of these issues and write a short paragraph on each.

A = Accuracy
B = Brevity
C = Clarity

Summary Report

After completion of a survey of 'My Own Place' as outlined, students may wish to consider writing a summary report on their findings, taking a specific aspect of the local area to focus on.

The **Summary Report** is a **core** item (i.e. compulsory) in the LCVP portfolio. It must be a word-processed document of 300–600 words. The emphasis in writing such a report must be in the ABC of effective communication – Accuracy, Brevity (brief) and Clarity.

There will be other opportunities to write summary reports within the LCVP, e.g. visitors to the classroom, a visit out or an investigation of a voluntary organisation. The portfolio layout for the summary report is set out below.

SUMMARY REPORT

REPORT on _____

For the attention of: (i.e. Teacher's name)

Prepared by: Your own name

Terms of Reference:
i.e. The instructions given to the report writer and/or include the aims of the activity here.

Introduction:
e.g. dates, duration, preparation beforehand. What is your involvement? etc.

Findings:
Outline of the main findings. Arrange the information in a logical sequence. Use bullet points or sequenced paragraphs.

Conclusion:
The conclusion should refer to the terms of reference and/or the aims of the report. The conclusion must also follow on as a result of the findings. Use bullet points if possible.

Recommendations:
The recommendations should be based on the conclusions. These might involve suggestions for future action, how a future investigation might be improved, follow-on classroom activities etc.

Note: In the section 'My Portfolio' there is a blank template on page 130 into which you can write your summary report, in preparation for typing the finished version.

Notes

The 'My Own Place' Report is an optional item for the LCVP portfolio. This is a more structured and in-depth report of 1,000–1,500 words. This will follow a more in-depth investigation of some aspect(s) of 'My Own Place'. We will look at this more formal report layout later in the book – also see 'My Portfolio' and 'LCVP Portfolio Guidelines'.

You cannot write a summary report on your local area and a 'My Own Place' report.

Additional notes

1. The title of the summary report should be clear and relevant, e.g. 'Report on Job Creation Agencies in our Area'.
2. The 'terms of reference' are the instructions given to the report writer, e.g. 'Write a report on the tourist potential of my local area and make recommendations on how existing attractions/facilities could be improved'. Alternatively, the student can use the heading 'Aims of the Activity'.
3. The findings should be presented in order of importance or in chronological order (i.e. in order of time/date). It is very important that the information is provided in a logical sequence.
4. The conclusion should refer back specifically to the aims and/or the terms of reference, e.g. were the aims achieved?
5. The recommendations should be appropriate to the aims/terms of reference, and should follow on logically from the conclusions. The recommendations may be dictated by the terms of reference (see above), or may be a follow-on to doing the investigation, e.g. recommendations to improve similar future investigations.

Warning

1. The Summary Report must be based on an LCVP-related activity.
2. No two portfolio items can be on the same activity (excl. an enterprise plan and a follow-on enterprise report or recorded interview).

Task

(a) Write a Summary Report on 'My Own Place' outlining either:
   * the potential for tourism in the local area; or
   * the main economic activities in the local area.
   Make one recommendation as to how the situation can be improved.

(b) Write a Summary Report on a Health & Safety survey of your school and make relevant recommendations.

(c) Role-play a situation that could give rise to a dispute in the workplace, e.g. looking for a pay rise. You should consider how the dispute can be resolved. (Remember that both sides are quite determined and have their own points of view.)

(d) Choose a local training scheme, or a scheme that assists the unemployed, and write a brief account (200 words) about it.

(e) With regard to **your** Leaving Certificate subjects, choose any three and state how each one is relevant to your chosen career or the world of work.

(f) If a person was unemployed, what financial benefits would the State provide?

(g) Name two trade unions. Explain three functions of a trade union.

2

Job-Seeking Skills

At the end of this chapter students should be able to (tick ✓ the box when completed):

* Recognise the different ways in which job vacancies are advertised. ☐

* Apply for a job by letter, telephone and e-mail. ☐

* Complete an application form. ☐

* Compile and create a curriculum vitae (CV). ☐

* Explain how to prepare for a job interview. ☐

* Engage in a simulated job interview. ☐

Job Vacancies

Businesses have to advertise job vacancies occasionally. There are a variety of reasons including the following.

* The business is expanding, and thus needs more employees.
* There may be seasonal work available, e.g. pre-Christmas shopping rush.
* Employees may be retiring.
* Employees may be leaving to go work elsewhere, or they may be fired for misconduct.
* Temporary workers may be needed to replace an employee on leave, e.g. maternity leave, sick leave.
* Contract workers may be needed to complete a specific job within a business, e.g. contract cleaners, computer maintenance.

Businesses use a variety of media to advertise the job vacancy. These include the following.

* **Newspapers**: national and local newspapers regularly advertise a wide variety of job vacancies. Some newspapers carry an 'appointments' section and/or a 'job vacancy' section on their website.
* **Local radio stations** often advertise local job vacancies.
* **Aertel and the teletext pages of other television stations** often have an employment section.
* **Internet**: job vacancies are often advertised on the website of a business. There are also job vacancy websites, e.g. www.irishjobs.ie.
* The **window/notice board** of local shops.
* A **notice board** within the business, especially if internal candidates are being sought.
* **Job recruitment exhibitions**.
* **Notice board in local colleges**.
* **Job recruitment agencies**: for a fee, the recruitment agency finds suitable candidates for job vacancies in client businesses.
* **Job training agencies**, e.g. FÁS.
* **Word of mouth**, especially for temporary positions, e.g. summer work.

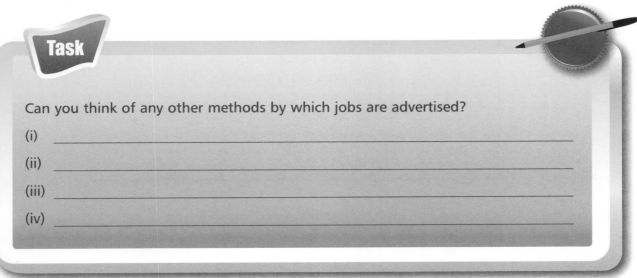

Task

Can you think of any other methods by which jobs are advertised?

(i) _____

(ii) _____

(iii) _____

(iv) _____

Websites
www.irishjobs.ie
www.fas.ie
www.monster.ie
www.jobs.ie
www.gumtree.ie
www.loadzajobs.ie
www.irishtimes.com
www.independent.ie
www.recruitmentagenciesireland.ie

Applying for a Job

When applying for a job, it is very important to read the advertisement carefully.

Shop Manager

A vacancy has arisen for the position of manager
of a large supermarket.

Suitable candidates must display leadership qualities, as well
as excellent communication and organisational skills.
IT skills are a requirement.
Candidates should possess a suitable management
qualification, as well as a minimum of 5 years relevant
experience.

Please apply in writing to the following address for an
application form.
**O'Reilly's Supermarket,
104 Pearse Ave.,
Roscrea, Co. Tipperary**.

Closing date for applications: 28 April 2011.
An Equal Opportunities Employer

Job advertisements will usually do the following.
* Describe the job briefly (including the principal duties).
* Outline the skills and qualities required from the candidate they are seeking.
* Refer to qualification and experience requirements.

The candidate will be invited to apply by the following means.
* Letter.
* Application form.
* Telephone.
* E-mail.
* On-line.

You may be asked to write a letter in the written examination.

Letter

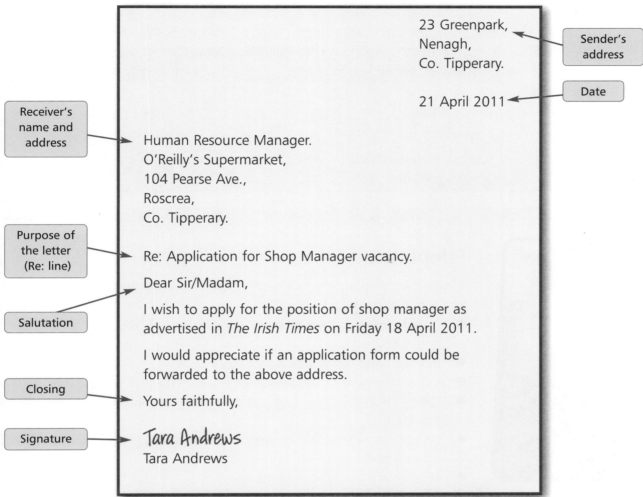

Sender's address

Date

Receiver's name and address

Human Resource Manager.
O'Reilly's Supermarket,
104 Pearse Ave.,
Roscrea,
Co. Tipperary.

23 Greenpark,
Nenagh,
Co. Tipperary.

21 April 2011

Purpose of the letter (Re: line)

Re: Application for Shop Manager vacancy.

Salutation

Dear Sir/Madam,

I wish to apply for the position of shop manager as advertised in *The Irish Times* on Friday 18 April 2011.

I would appreciate if an application form could be forwarded to the above address.

Closing

Yours faithfully,

Signature

Tara Andrews
Tara Andrews

Notes

1. Always be careful with spellings, grammar and punctuation. Use short and concise sentences (Accurate, Brief, Clear).
2. The 'salutation' (greeting) should use the person's name if it is known, i.e. Dear Ms O'Brien or Dear Mr Ryan. If you know the person's name, then the 'closing' should be 'Yours sincerely', although 'Yours faithfully' is acceptable.

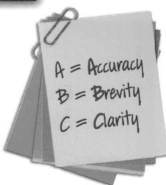

A = Accuracy
B = Brevity
C = Clarity

Notes

Qualities and Skills
Qualities – the characteristics that you were born with or developed as you grew up, e.g. honesty.

Skills – the talents that you have acquired or developed over time, through training or practice, e.g. computer skills, communication skills etc.

Choose an advertisement for a job vacancy from a local or a national newspaper.

(i) Identify one quality (characteristic) and one skill being looked for in the candidate. If none are mentioned, then name one quality and one skill that would be relevant to the job.

(ii) Write a letter, using today's date, asking for an application form and further details of the vacancy (do not post it).

(iii) Name two other media where this job could be advertised and give a different reason why each would be suitable.

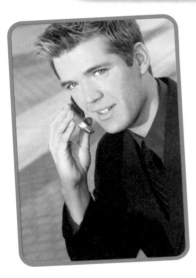

Telephone

If invited to telephone for an application form or to make an appointment, first consider the following.

* Prepare what you are going to say beforehand. You do not want to forget anything.
* Be polite and speak clearly.
* Know the name of the person or department that you are looking for.
* Have a pen and paper ready to take down any information and details provided.
* Do not hesitate to ask the person to repeat any information that you have missed.
* Be sure to provide your name and contact details.

The telephone can also be used to obtain information about an organisation prior to attending an interview. Names, details about the organisation (including its product or service range), publicity brochures etc. could be requested.

E-mail

To: oreillysroscrea@eircom.net
From: tandrews2@gmail.com
Cc:
Subject: Shop manager vacancy application
Attachments: none

Dear Sir/Madam,

I wish to apply for the position of shop manager as advertised in the *Irish Independent* on Friday 18 April 2011. I would appreciate if an application form could be forwarded to: 23 Greenpark, Nenagh, Co. Tipperary.

Yours faithfully,
Tara Andrews

Cc: = carbon copy. This is used if you wish to send the e-mail to a number of people.
Subject = the purpose or content of the e-mail. Without a recognisable 'subject', many people will not open the e-mail due to the risk of a virus. You must know the e-mail address of the recipient.

Note: e-mails are not confidential and should not contain private information.

E-mail should only be used if it is stated in the advertisement. Many of the same guidelines for letter writing and using the telephone can also be used here, e.g. use short concise sentences, be polite, provide contact details etc. Your e-mail address will be sent automatically.

E-mails can also be used to request information about the organisation.

Application Form

Many organisations provide an application form for job vacancies. The application form may contain some of the following sections.

* Personal details, e.g. name, address etc.
* Education details, e.g. schools/colleges attended, qualifications.
* Work experience details, e.g. part-time jobs.
* Skills and qualities that you have to offer, e.g. why do you believe you are a suitable candidate for the job?
* Goals/ambitions, e.g. what do you want to achieve?
* Referees, i.e. the name of at least one person who will provide you with a reference, outlining why you are suitable for the position and the type of person you are.

When completing an application form, make sure that you **read the instructions**. For example, you may be requested to use BLOCK CAPITAL LETTERS or a **black** or a **blue** pen.

It is a good idea to begin by photocopying the form and filling in a copy first for practice. Refine your answers so that you get across what you want to say. You should complete all of the sections. If a section does not apply to you, write 'not applicable' or 'n/a' or draw a line through the section. Do not leave any blank spaces. It might appear that you were unable to answer the question or that you were careless.

You should also take the following steps when completing an application form.
* Take note of the closing date and ensure that you return the application form in plenty of time.
* Read your answers carefully for mistakes, misspellings and omissions. If possible, ask somebody else to proof-read it for you.
* Photocopy the application form prior to returning it. You will most likely be asked for details about your answers during an interview.
* If any additional documentation is requested, ensure that photocopies of these documents are enclosed, e.g. driving licence, education certificates etc.
* Ask for a certificate of posting at the post office.
* If requested to send the original of an important document, it is advisable to use a hard envelope and register the letter.

Complete the following application form, using your own personal details.

Application Form

Please complete all sections.

Name: _____

Present Address: _____

Telephone No.: _____

Home Address (if not as above): _____

Date of Birth: _____

Do you hold an EU passport: Yes/No _____

Do you require a work permit to work in Ireland: Yes/No _____

Education

	Name of Schools or Colleges	Years From	To	Examination Taken	Results
Second Level					
Third Level					
Training Courses Attended					

Interests/Hobbies

_____

_____

_____

_____

_____

_____

Have you previously been employed by this company? Yes/No _____

If yes, please give details.

_____

_____

For applicants under 18 years of age, if you do not live with your parents please state the name of the person you live with:

_____

At what times are you available to work?

Full time ☐ Please Specify: _____

Part time ☐ Please Specify: _____

Previous Employment Record

List your present/most recent employment first. NB. It is important that all previous employment is included.

Dates (to/from)	Name, Address and Telephone Number of Employer	Position Held and Rate of Pay	Reason for Leaving

Personal References

Please give the details of two people we may contact for references, one being a previous employer if possible; no relatives.

Name: _____   Name: _____
Address: _____   Address: _____
_____   _____
_____   _____
Telephone: _____   Telephone: _____
Position: _____   Position: _____

Health

Have you consulted a doctor/attended a hospital or received any treatment for back problems, or for skin trouble of any kind? Yes/No _____
If yes, please give details.

_____

_____

Have you ever been injured in an accident at work or elsewhere? Yes/No _____
If yes, please give details.

_____

_____

Declaration

I certify that the foregoing is a full list of my former employers. I agree that _____ (name of company) are at liberty to contact all or any such former employers for references about me. I accept that communication between (name of company) and my former employers and replies from such employers are privileged and will not be disclosed to me. I declare that the above information is complete and correct.

Signature: _____   Date: _____

Application Forms

Other than job application forms, there are a wide variety of application forms, and other forms, that you will need to complete as part of daily life. Examples include: application for tax credits (P21); application for a driving licence; insurance proposal form; application for a club membership; bank account application form and so on. The same care and procedures should be followed as outlined.

Task

Obtain an application form, or some other form, and complete it. (Application forms may be available from local businesses or clubs, or can be downloaded from the Internet, e.g. www.revenue.ie).

Curriculum Vitae

The curriculum vitae (CV) is a summary of the details of your life to date, including your skills and achievements. It is given to a prospective employer so as to entice him/her to give you a job. The layout of a CV can vary, but the following layout is currently in line with the LCVP marking scheme.

Note: This is a compulsory portfolio item.

CURRICULUM VITAE

PERSONAL DETAILS

Surname:

First Name:

Address:

Telephone No.:

EDUCATIONAL DETAILS

Dates	Primary School Name & Address
Dates	Secondary School Name & Address

EXAMINATION DETAILS
Junior Certificate (Date)

Subjects	Level	Grade

Leaving Certificate (Date)

Subjects	Level	Grade

WORK EXPERIENCE

Dates	Name of Organisation	Position/Role

> Briefly describe your duties and/or responsibilities. Must be the work experience undertaken as part of the LCVP.

INTERESTS & HOBBIES

-
-
-
-

> Short sentences – do not use single words.

ACHIEVEMENTS

-
-
-
-

SKILLS & QUALITIES

-
-
-
-

REFEREES

> Include title e.g. Mr, Ms, Fr.

Name: _____   Name: _____

Job Title: _____   Job Title: _____

Address: _____   Address: _____

_____   _____

_____   _____

_____   _____

Telephone: _____   Telephone: _____

Signature: _____   Date: _____

(Name printed)

The following points should be noted regarding the CV layout for the LCVP.

* The CV must be **word processed** for the LCVP portfolio.
* It must not exceed **2 pages** in length.
* There should be **two referees**. (A referee is a person [non-relative] who is prepared to give you a good recommendation regarding your suitability for the job.)

  The entry for a referee should look like this:
  Mr Thomas Carroll
  Principal
  St. Mary's Secondary School
  Cobh
  Co. Cork.
  Tel. (021) 123456

* LCVP **must** be entered as a Leaving Certificate subject correctly named as **Link Modules**.
* The **subject level** should be entered as Higher (H), Ordinary (O) or Common (C).
* For **skills & qualities** you may use a short statement summarising your main qualities and skills, instead of the bulleted list. The statement would usually appear at the top of the CV. The statement should be carefully phrased and preferably highlighted.

Note: In the section 'My Portfolio' there is a blank template on page 132 into which you can write your CV, in preparation for typing the finished version.

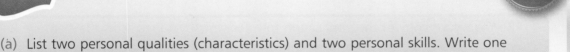

Task

(a) List two personal qualities (characteristics) and two personal skills. Write one sentence describing **each**.

(b) Identify at least one of your achievements to date, e.g. sport's award.

(c) Complete your curriculum vitae (CV).

Websites
www.cvtips.com
www.irishjobs.ie
www.qualifax.ie
www.labsupport.ie
www.interviewtechniques.ie
www.alec.co.uk
www.measurability.ie
www.cvtemplate.net
www.interviewsolutions.ie

Job Interview

The employer may have been impressed by your CV or application form, but will want to find out more about you in an interview before giving you the job. It is very important that you are prepared when you are invited to attend for the interview.

In preparing for a job interview you should take the following steps.

> Take note of the **date**, **time** and **place** of the interview – you do not want to miss the interview or be late.
> If you are unsure about the venue, or how to get there, then it is important that you make all the necessary arrangements in plenty of time.

> **Dress** appropriately and neatly.

> **Research** the business and the position that you are applying for. Make use of the Internet, telephone and business contacts. If possible, try to speak to somebody in a similar job.

> **Re-read** your copy of the application form or your CV to refresh your memory. Be prepared to answer questions about information you have given, and be prepared to provide additional information or back-up material, e.g. copies of certificates.

> Know your **qualities and skills**, especially those that apply to this job. Concentrate on getting these across to the employer during the interview.

> Prepare any **documentation** that you have been asked to bring with you.

> **Prepare answers to questions** that you feel are likely to be asked – see the sample questions on the next page. Research and prepare your answers. Ask a friend/relative to interview you, and practise your answers.

> **Prepare any questions** that you want to ask about the job or the organisation, as you will usually be provided with an opportunity to ask questions. Keep the questions short and relevant.

> Get there **early**, and remember to be on your **best behaviour** from the moment that you enter the building – you don't know who is watching.

During the interview:

* Maintain eye contact with the person asking the question (there may be more than one interviewer).
* Listen carefully to the question. If you are unsure, ask for it to be repeated. Answer each part of the question.
* Sit upright and do not fidget. Body language can influence the interviewer(s).
* If you do not know the answer to a question, you are usually better off admitting this rather than bluffing and getting caught out.
* Try to relax and be confident – you will be if you have prepared well.
* Be polite and thank the interviewer(s).

For some senior positions in an organisation you may be asked to make a short presentation on a selected topic. If so, have your material ready for an overhead projector or use 'powerpoint' on a data projector (with a notebook computer), whichever is available. Prepare your material in a logical sequence, speak slowly and clearly, and be concise. (See Chapter 5.)

Sample Interview Questions

The interviewer(s) will normally begin by asking you questions based on your application form/curriculum vitae, e.g. educational details, hobbies and interests, achievements etc. The interviewer(s) will then proceed to more in-depth questions.

Here is a short list of sample questions.

* In your work experience, what were your duties and responsibilities?
* How do you feel you related with your colleagues?
* In giving you this job, what skills and/or qualities will you bring to the position?
* What do you believe are your strengths and/or weaknesses?
* What skills or qualities do you believe are essential for this position and why?
* What makes you believe you can work well as part of a team?
* What qualities and/or skills are needed, in your opinion, to work as part of a team?
* What would you like to achieve from this job if successful?
* Where do you see yourself in five years time?
* How did you deal with a difficult situation in your previous employment or how would you deal with a hypothetical problem in this job? (The interviewer poses the difficult problem.)

Task

(a) Working in pairs, prepare five questions for a job interview and then prepare the answers to these questions.

(b) Working in groups of three students, role play a job interview. Each student should take turns being the interviewer, the interviewee and the observer.

(c) (i) Write a letter, on today's date, applying for this job.

(ii) Identify two skills and two qualities that you believe are needed for this job.

(iii) Name two other methods by which this job could have been advertised.

(iv) Identify three steps that you should take if called for an interview for this position.

Sales Assistant
Full-time

Required for large TV & Electrical Store.

Retail experience an advantage.
Applicants should be self-motivated and have good communication skills.

A letter of application, together with a current curriculum vitae, should be sent to:
**The Manager,
Electrical Superstore Ltd,
Westgate Retail Park, Limerick.**

An Equal Opportunities Employer

(d) Working in groups of three students, role play a telephone call requesting an application form to be forwarded to you. Use the above advertisement or select a job advertisement. (The role play could also be recorded on audio tape or video, as preparation for future portfolio material.)

(e) (i) Explain the term 'equal opportunities employer'.

(ii) Outline three methods that an employer may use to recruit employees.

(iii) Give two reasons why you think good IT skills are important for the workplace.

(iv) Describe briefly two ways that you can show an interviewer that you have good communication skills.

(f) A mini-enterprise has been set up in your school. It is a mini-company producing 'hoodies' with a school logo/crest. The mini-company has advertised three positions: designer, marketing manager and production manager.

   (i) Choose one of the positions advertised and describe the skills and experience that you would highlight in your curriculum vitae if you were applying for that position.

   (ii) What does the word 'referee' mean on a curriculum vitae?

   (iii) List two questions that might be asked at an interview for the position you have chosen and write a short reply to each question.

Vacancy

Enterprising person to join a marketing team.
Computer and keyboarding skills essential.
Apply with a Curriculum Vitae
to:
The Human Resources Manager,
Tower Ltd,
Westport, Co. Mayo.

(g) (i) Name three advertising media where the above advertisement could be placed. Give one reason for each of the media you have named.

   (ii) Why are applicants asked to list referees, or provide references, on their curriculum vitae?

   (iii) Why do you think Tower Ltd want an enterprising person?

   (iv) Outline three ways you consider a successful applicant could be enterprising in this job.

(h) (i) Write a letter applying for the position advertised in the previous question.

   (ii) List two qualities and two skills that you feel would give you an advantage when applying for this position. Give a reason for each of your choices.

   (iii) Briefly describe four steps that you would take in preparing for an interview.

3

Career Investigation

At the end of this chapter students should be able to (tick ✓ the box when completed):

* Identify personal aptitudes and interests. ☐

* Investigate a range of careers appropriate to personal aptitude and interests. ☐

* Identify and analyse the aptitude and skills required to pursue a specific career. ☐

* Describe the relevant qualifications and training required for entry to the selected career. ☐

* Identify the available opportunities to pursue a selected career locally, nationally and, where possible, at an international level. ☐

* Plan and set up an opportunity to interview and/or work shadow a person in a selected career. ☐

* Integrate information from a variety of sources to prepare a final report on a career investigation. ☐

* Reflect on and evaluate the experience of undertaking a career investigation. ☐

* Link the activities in this unit to learning in the relevant Leaving Certificate subjects. ☐

Student Profile

It is strongly advisable that students begin a career investigation by undertaking a study of your own interests, work experience, qualities (characteristics), skills and aptitudes. Students also need to consider their subject choices. Based on these findings, they should then be in a better position to choose a suitable career for an investigation.

It is useful to make a detailed list of all your interests etc. using the following headings, which are dealt with below.

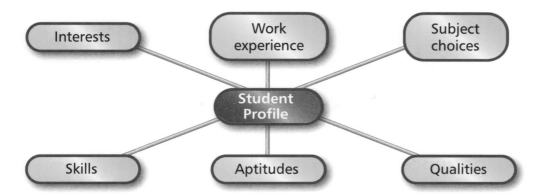

Interests

* Sports, e.g. swimming, soccer, walking, running etc.
* Hobbies, e.g. listening to music, dancing, photography.
* An interest in computers, surfing the Internet, cars etc.
* Achievements, e.g. certificate for typing, speech & drama, first aid etc.

Subject Choices

The subjects that a student has chosen may have a bearing on his/her career choice. For some courses a particular subject or subjects may be compulsory – for example a science subject for nursing, higher level maths for actuary etc.

A chosen subject may also reflect a particular interest or aptitude (ability) of the student and may indicate a possible career choice, e.g. accountancy (accountant), music, art etc.

Other examples include:
* Art – graphic designer, artist, fashion designer etc.
* Science subjects – doctor, nurse, vet, dentist, laboratory technician, physiotherapist etc.
* Maths – engineer, actuary, physicist etc.
* Construction Studies – carpenter, electrician etc.
* Engineering – engineer, architect etc.
* Languages – tourist industry, interpreter, call centre staff, translator etc.
* Home Economics – chef, hotel manager, child care worker, nurse, management etc.
* Business subjects – entrepreneur, accountant, production manager etc.

It is very important that students consult their **Career Guidance** teacher for more up-to-date information regarding subject choices.

Task

(a) Identify one career path that could be associated with each of your Leaving Certificate subjects.

(b) In your opinion, what Leaving Certificate subjects would be beneficial, or required, for each of the following careers: (i) solicitor; (ii) secretary; (iii) Garda; and (iv) beautician?

Work Experience

Many 5th year students have had some level of work experience. For example:

* Casual work, e.g. babysitting, working in the family business etc.
* Part-time work.
* Work experience in transition year.
* Work experience as part of the LCVP.

As a result, the student may have identified a career that he/she would like, or their likes/dislikes associated with a particular career, e.g. working outdoors, working with children etc. For more information on work experience, see Chapter 4.

Skills

No profile would be worthwhile without identifying your skills, i.e. those talents that you have acquired over time through training or practice. (It can also be a good idea to ask friends or relations to help in identifying your skills.)

You may also wish to categorise your skills as follows.

* **Practical skills** – cooking, letter writing, money management etc.
* **Technical skills** – driving, computer skills, telephone skills etc.
* **Language skills** – foreign language, communication skills etc.
* **Interpersonal (group) skills** – listening skills, teamwork skills, teaching skills, leadership etc.
* **Personal skills** – organising, time management, planning etc.

Task

Identify two skills that apply to you under each category in the following table. (Do not repeat a skill in other categories.)

Practical skills	Technical skills	Language skills	Interpersonal skills	Personal skills

Qualities

These are the characteristics that you were born with or that developed as you grew up. Qualities could include the following.

* Honest.
* Dependable.
* Self-motivated.
* Hard-working.

* Sociable.
* Work well with others.
* Confident.
* Leadership.

* Creative.
* Determined.
* Risk-taker.
* Ambitious.

Task

Identify five qualities that apply to you.

	Quality
1.	
2.	
3.	
4.	
5.	

Aptitudes

These are the areas (abilities) that you are usually good at. The Career Guidance teacher may give students a differential aptitude test in order to identify these abilities. Once identified, these abilities may point a person towards a certain career.

The differential aptitude test usually measures:

* Verbal reasoning.
* Numerical ability.
* Abstract reasoning.

* Clerical speed and accuracy.
* Mechanical reasoning.

* Space relations.
* Spelling.
* Language usage.

The Career Guidance teacher can advise you as the suitable careers for different aptitudes, e.g. numerical ability – accountancy, actuary etc.

Career Investigation

As part of the LCVP portfolio, students **must** undertake a career investigation. In this investigation, the student must take a specific career of his or her choice and examine the career under a variety of headings. The career investigation should be between 300 and 600 words and be in the form of a word processed document. (The student may produce a 3–5 minute career investigation interview on audiotape instead.)

Suggested Layout of a Career Investigation

Name of career.	**CAREER INVESTIGATION on** _____
	Prepared by:
Describe the career & the duties involved.	**Description:**
Must include two pathways to the selected career.	**Qualifications and Training Required:**
Should give five skills & qualities needed for this career.	**Relevant Skills and Qualities:**
Give details, e.g. name of interviewee. Give some positive and negative aspects of the career.	**Out of Class Learning Experience:**
Refer to all three areas in your answer. Is this the career for you?	**Evaluation of Career in Light of Personal Aptitudes, Interests and Choice of Leaving Certificate Subjects:**
You should evaluate what you learned about the career **and** about doing a career investigation, e.g. research skills, communication skills, positive/negative aspects of the career, different pathway options.	**Evaluation of Career Investigation:**
	Signed: _____ Date: _____

Note: In the section 'My Portfolio' there is a blank template on page 134 into which you can write your Career Investigation, in preparation for typing the finished version.

Notes on the Career Investigation

Pathways
You must identify **two** different ways of becoming qualified in the chosen career.

Pathway A	Pathway B
Location of course/training.	Location of course/training.
Entry requirements.	Entry requirements.
Length of course/training.	Length of course/training.
Qualification achieved.	Qualification achieved.

If the two pathways are very similar, e.g. two college courses, then you should highlight any differences that exist, e.g. course content, length, qualification, points required etc.

If the chosen career has only one pathway, e.g. Garda or army, then you should use 'Pathway B' to describe either a related career pathway in the same area of work, e.g. forensic science, or an alternative career pathway while waiting for acceptance or if unsuccessful.

Relevant skills and qualities
You must identify at least **two** skills and **two** qualities that you believe are relevant to working in this career.

Evaluation
You should identify those aptitudes and skills that you possess which you believe make you suitable to pursue this career, e.g. 'clerical speed and accuracy' for becoming a secretary/ receptionist. You should also identify those Leaving Certificate subjects, which you have chosen, that are required or beneficial for this career. Finally, you should also identify why your interests have pointed you in the direction of this career, e.g. working with children, working with computers etc.

Out of class learning experience
When researching this career, it is required that you interact with an adult, other than your teacher, concerning this career. You might interview a person involved in your chosen career or even work shadow them for a period of time. You should give details about the interview/work shadow, e.g. date(s), job title of the interviewee etc. You should also state what you have learned, e.g. benefits and/or drawbacks associated with the career. (Could be part of a visit to a careers exhibition.)

Evaluation of career investigation

You should identify the following.

* What you learned about the career, e.g. the existence of alternative pathways, does it suit your interests/subject choices etc.
* The quality and quantity of information gathered – did you have enough information to make an informed decision? Are you satisfied with the findings?
* Is this the career for you? Are you motivated to study harder?
* The skills gained and/or developed and the knowledge gained by undertaking such research.

Note

You **must not** copy or download any information directly into your investigation, other than career pathway details (e.g. course details). Where you refer to or quote from a brochure/ website/text, you should give this reference at the end of your investigation, i.e. name of brochure/website/text, author's name. Do **not** copy the brochure/website/text.

Audio Interview

This is only recommended if word processing is not possible.

If you are considering undertaking the career investigation as an audio interview, the following points should be noted.

* It is the **student** that must be interviewed about the career of his/her choice.
* The interview must be 3–5 minutes in duration.
* The student must communicate in a clear and confident manner.
* The same **criteria and headings** will apply in this interview, i.e. the same questions must be answered.
* The student's **name and exam number** must be identified.

Interview questions could include the following.

(a) What is your name and examination number?
(b) What career did you choose to investigate as part of the LCVP?
(c) Briefly describe '*name the career*'.
(d) What skills and qualities do you believe you would need to pursue a career in …?
(e) What training, and qualification, would you require for this career? (Give the details of two pathways.)
(f) Why did you choose to investigate this career?
(g) Outside of school, what did you do to research this career and what did you find out?
(h) What did you learn about the career and yourself from undertaking this career investigation?

 Remember: you should give the same answers as you would give if doing the word processed document, as the same marking scheme will be used.

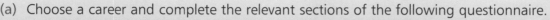

Task

(a) Choose a career and complete the relevant sections of the following questionnaire.

Name of Course:	College:	Points (this year):	Qualification:

Contact Person:	Course Duration:	Entry Requirements:	Additional Information:

Course Content or Modules:	Information Learned Regarding the Career:

(b) Now research a **second pathway** to the **same** career. Copy the above questionnaire into your answer book and answer the questions for this pathway.

Employment in Ireland has changed in recent years in many ways, including the following aspects.

* Immigration, as workers from abroad came into Ireland to avail of employment opportunities.
* High labour costs have resulted in semi-skilled, labour-intensive industries closing or moving abroad.
* High unemployment as a result of the recession, and a scarcity of employment opportunities in Ireland.
* Emigration, as people leave Ireland to find work abroad.
* Changes in employment legislation have given workers more protection and rights.
* Many workers are now employed as contract workers or as part-time workers.

Identifying Opportunities to Pursue a Career

✳ Local or national newspapers usually have a recruitment section where you can see the range of job opportunities available – skills and qualities are often mentioned.

✳ Websites such as www.unison.ie and www.irishjobs.ie will also display a wide range of employment opportunities.

✳ Recruitment agencies can also advise on employment prospects, and help place a candidate in employment (for a fee).

✳ Careers exhibitions and open days highlight employment opportunities.

✳ Media, such as television and radio, occasionally advertise job vacancies.

✳ Interviewing a person currently involved in a career will usually help to identify career opportunities and prospects.

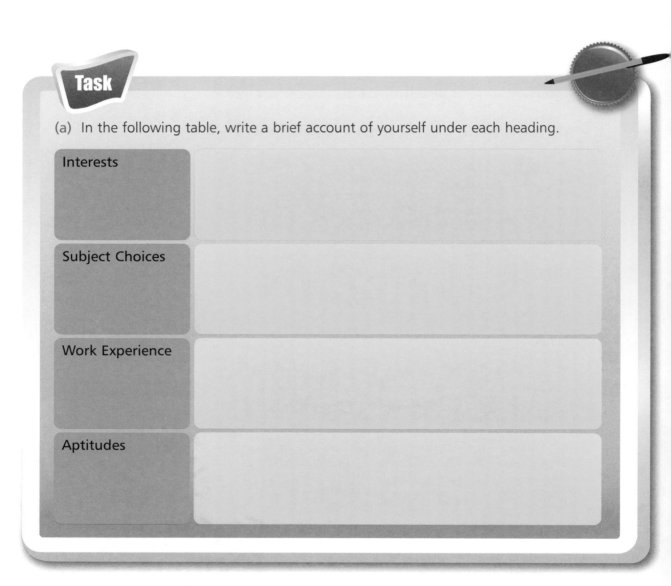

Task

(a) In the following table, write a brief account of yourself under each heading.

Interests	
Subject Choices	
Work Experience	
Aptitudes	

Task

(b) In the following table, write **two** skills and **two** qualities that you would associate with a person in the chosen career.

Career	Skills	Qualities
Nurse	1. 2.	1. 2.
Solicitor	1. 2.	1. 2.
Teacher	1. 2.	1. 2.
Mechanic	1. 2.	1. 2.
Farmer	1. 2.	1. 2.
Hairdresser	1. 2.	1. 2.

(c) Name **two** careers that you would associate with each of the following aptitudes.

Aptitude	Career	Career
Numerical ability		
Mechanical reasoning		
Language usage		
Abstract reasoning		

(d) Prepare **six** questions to ask when interviewing a person in a selected career.

(i) _____

(ii) _____

(iii) _____

(iv) _____

(v) _____

(vi) _____

Task

(e) In undertaking the career investigation activity:
  (i)   What did you learn about the career that you did not know before?
  (ii) List two positive and two negative points about the career that you investigated.
  (iii) What skills did you acquire, or improve, by undertaking this investigation?
  (iv) List two ways in which you benefited by completing this career investigation.

(f) Answer the following questions in your copy book.
  (i)   What career would you like to pursue after you leave school?
  (ii) What training and/or qualification is required for this career?
  (iii) What is the current salary scale for this career? What is the starting wage?
  (iv) Name two skills and two qualities that you believe would be needed in this career.

(g) (i)   You have been asked to complete a career investigation on a job of your choice. Present your findings as a poster (or web page) giving at least six items of information.
  (ii) Describe two changes that have taken place in employment in Ireland in the last five years.
  (iii) List three characteristics that employers might look for in potential employees. Give one reason why **each** characteristic might be considered important.

4

Work Placement

At the end of this chapter students should be able to (tick ✓ the box when completed):

* Specify personal goals in relation to a work placement. ☐

* Plan and organise a work placement. ☐

* Attend punctually for a specific placement. ☐

* Dress appropriately for a specific placement. ☐

* Follow a set of procedures in accordance with specific instructions. ☐

* Communicate effectively with other workers in a
  particular placement. ☐

* Follow a specific set of instructions relating to Health and Safety. ☐

* Review personal experiences in relation to a work placement. ☐

* Analyse reports by adults of personal performance in a workplace. ☐

* Reflect on and evaluate a specific work placement in the light
  of career aspirations. ☐

* Describe how what has been learned can be applied to work
  at home, in school and in the community. ☐

* Present a diary/written/verbal report on a specific work placement. ☐

* Link the activities in this unit to learning in relevant
  Leaving Certificate subjects. ☐

In this unit you are expected to plan, organise and undertake a **work experience placement** or a **work shadowing placement**.

Work experience involves being at work in a workplace and completing assigned duties so as to experience a taste of the career.

Work shadowing involves the student observing or 'shadowing' a person undertaking a particular job.

Work Experience and Work Shadowing

Work experience allows students to:

* Experience the workplace, e.g. duties, interacting with the public.
* Experience their chosen career or a related career activity, e.g. working with children.
* Develop and/or learn skills, e.g. filing, dealing with the public, applying for the job.
* Develop social skills associated with the workplace, e.g. teamwork, meeting people.
* Identify personal interests and aptitudes.
* Relate the experience to their subject choices and possible career paths.
* Gain an insight into whether they like the career or not.

Work shadowing allows students to:

* Observe and investigate certain careers that they would not be able to work at first-hand, e.g. solicitor, architect, doctor.
* Develop their communication, investigative and research skills.
* Relate the experience to their subject choices and possible career paths.
* Develop social skills associated with the workplace, e.g. interacting with work colleagues, interacting with the public.
* Identify personal interests and aptitudes.

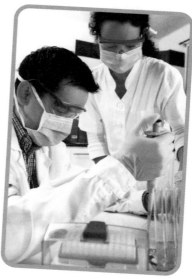

Note: The above points could, and should, form part of the evaluation of the work experience – both on a daily basis and as part of the overall evaluation.

In organising your work experience/work shadowing, it is very important that you identify the **reason(s) why you have chosen this placement**, and link these to your possible career choice, skills and aptitudes, personal interests, subject choices etc. (see 'Career Investigation' on page 38). You should also identify the skills and experiences that you hope to acquire by undertaking this placement.

When completing the 'Diary of Work Experience' in the portfolio (an optional portfolio item), you are required to explain the reason(s) for your choice of work placement.

Finding Work Experience/Work Shadowing

When looking for a work placement, you should do the following.

* Decide on the career and/or experience that you would like.
* Identify the businesses in your locality that would be suitable, e.g. a primary school or crèche for childcare.
* Write a letter to, telephone or personally visit the business to ask if they would be willing to accommodate your work placement.
* Ask family members or relatives as they may have contacts that could be of assistance.
* Ask your LCVP teacher as he/she will be able to offer advice and may be of assistance.

Finding the work placement is, in itself, a great experience and should help you to develop a range of skills and experiences, such as:

* Identifying and researching placement opportunities.
* Applying for a work placement by post, telephone or in person.
* Preparing and sending a letter of application and/or curriculum vitae (CV).
* Being interviewed for the placement.
* Liaising between the employer and the school, e.g. insurance cover, teacher visitation.
* Accepting responsibility for planning and organising the placement, travel arrangements, etc.
* Dealing with disappointments.

Task

(a) Name a career that you would like to learn more about through work experience/ work shadowing.

_____

Give two reasons why you chose this career.

(i) _____

(ii) _____

(b) Name two of your subjects that are relevant or required for this career, and explain the reason why in each case.

Subject 1: _____

_____

_____

Subject 2: _____

_____

_____

(c) Identify two skills and two qualities (characteristics) that you believe would be required for your chosen career.

Skills	Qualities
1.	1.
2.	2.

Guidelines for Work Placement

* Know the starting and finishing times of the working day and ensure that you attend punctually.
* Observe the dress code and always dress appropriately.
* Identify your job description and the duties attached.
* Follow the instructions given.
* Observe the Health and Safety guidelines of the workplace (see 'Introduction to Working Life' on page 8).
* Maintain the confidentiality of the workplace.
* Treat people with respect and courtesy.
* Use your initiative when performing tasks.
* If asked to perform a task that you deem to be unsafe or inappropriate, notify the supervisor politely and explain your reason. Ask if you can perform another task. If dissatisfied, inform your teacher/school/parent.
* If you are harassed/bullied, tell the supervisor or any other senior person in the organisation immediately. If dissatisfied, tell your teacher/school/parent.
* If you are unable to attend, notify the work placement immediately and apologise. Then inform your teacher and/or school of your absence.

Work Experience Diary

The diary is one of four **optional** items that make up the LCVP Portfolio. You must complete two optional items. The diary must be between 1,000 and 1,500 words and be either hand-written or word processed. The diary will be an account of your activities, observations and insights (evaluation) while on work experience. It should contain a minimum of three dated entries in chronological order.

For work shadowing, the diary can relate your in-school preparations, your work shadowing experiences and observations, and your evaluation of the placement. (The work shadowing placement may be for a shorter period – see Department of Education & Science guidelines.)

Recorded Interview

The recorded interview (video) is another portfolio option whereby you can be interviewed regarding your work experience/work shadowing. However, you should take careful note of the following.

* The recorded interview option has a different marking scheme to the diary – see the portfolio guidelines and marking scheme on page 127.
* No two portfolio items can be on the same topic/activity, excluding the enterprise plan ('before') and the enterprise report ('after').

You cannot submit a 'Recorded Interview' and 'Diary' on your work placement.

Possible Diary Layout

Page 1

WORK EXPERIENCE DIARY

Name of Workplace: _____

Description of Workplace: _____

_____

_____

_____

_____

Reason(s) for Choosing this Placement: _____

_____

_____

_____

Dates: _____

Summary of Duties: _____

_____

_____

_____

_____

_____

Give 2–3 reasons for choosing this placement, relevant to a career, subjects, aptitudes, skills that you are hoping to acquire, etc.

Pages 2–6
There should be one page for each day of work experience, or preparation, shadowing and feedback on work shadowing. There must be a minimum of three days or entries.

STUDENT WORK DIARY

Day: _____ Date: _____ Name of Supervisor: _____

What I did at work today. _____

_____

_____

What new thing did I learn today? _____

_____

_____

The main problems I experienced today. _____

_____

_____

> Did you experience problems, and how did you deal with them?

What I found most interesting. _____

_____

_____

How did I relate with others? _____

> How you got on with customers and work colleagues.

_____

_____

Evaluation of today. _____

> Beneficial – Yes/No? Why? Give reasons.

_____

_____

_____

Page 7

Evaluation

Evaluate the placement with regard to further study and career aspirations.

> How did you get on? Is this the career and/or organisation for you?

_____

_____

_____

_____

_____

Skills/experiences acquired or improved. _____

_____

_____

_____

Evaluate how what has been learned can be applied in the home, school and community.

> Make sure that you write a sentence about each of the three areas.

_____

_____

_____

_____

_____

_____

_____

_____

Notes on the Evaluation

Career

Refer to the reasons why this placement is relevant to your career choice, for example:

* This is the career path that you still want to follow.
* You are now motivated to study harder to achieve your goal.
* It is not the career for you, but it presented you with relevant skills and experiences.
* This was an important introduction to the world of work.

Skills

Identify the skills acquired or developed during the placement. (You can refer to personal skills/ aptitudes and interests.)

Home/School/Community

How has the work placement, and the skills and knowledge acquired/developed, affected your attitude, behaviour or participation at home, in school and in your community? For example, are you more focused on study and your career pathway? Are you more aware of your parents' responsibilities and workload – do you help out more at home? Have you become more involved with community groups and organisations – acquiring experience or sharing your skills?

Important Points Regarding Your Work Placement

* Organise your work experience/shadowing in plenty of time.
* Students are usually covered by the school insurance policy for work experience, subject to certain terms and conditions of the policy. Your teacher will check the details.
* Work on a building site (however brief) requires a health and safety certificate ('Safe Pass') which involves training and a fee.
* Consent forms are required from parents/guardians for insurance purposes.
* Present your Employer Report Form – it is usual, and expected, to give the employer a form to complete so as to record his/her feedback (see the next page).
* Keep a diary of your activities each day, including tasks performed, names, dates and evaluation. Otherwise relevant details can be easily forgotten.

Sample Employer Report Form

EMPLOYER REPORT FORM

Name of School: _____

Student's Name: _____

Name & Address of Work Placement: _____

_____

Dates: _____   Contact Person: _____

Please tick (✓) as appropriate

	Excellent	Good	Fair	Poor
Punctuality				
Ability to complete tasks set				
Ability to work on own initiative				
Appropriate dress				
Ability to relate to other members of the workforce				
Quality of work				
Reliability				
Interest shown in the career				

Additional Comments: _____

_____

_____

Employer/Supervisor Signature: _____ Date: _____

The feedback obtained from a report like this should be examined carefully and any praise or criticism noted for future reference. This feedback can also be incorporated into the diary or video. (A photocopy of the report itself can be included in the portfolio as an appendix.)

Task

(a) Name a career of your choice and list three suitable work placements relevant to this career.

(b) Write a letter to an employer of your choice requesting one week's work experience or a work shadowing arrangement, using today's date. Use your school's name and address.

(c) (i) Distinguish between work experience and work shadowing.
  (ii) Outline two benefits of both work experience and work shadowing, as you see them.

(d) Identify four ways in which work experience differs from school work.

(e) Name three Health and Safety features and/or procedures that you observed while undertaking your work placement.

(f) Evaluate your own work experience with particular reference to each of the following.
  (i) Relevance to your preferred career path.
  (ii) Relevance to your subjects and to your interests or aptitudes.
  (iii) Relevance to the 'world of work'.
  (iv) Skills and/or knowledge acquired or improved.
  (v) How the experience benefited you: in your school work; at home; and in your local community.

(g) What difficulties did you experience, and how did you deal with them, in the following situations.
  (i) Finding work experience/work shadowing?
  (ii) Participating in your work placement?

(h) (i) Give two reasons why you would consider it important that an employee should have clearly defined tasks and responsibilities in the workplace?
  (ii) List three ways of finding work experience. Give one advantage for each.

(i) Describe, in detail, two ways in which your work placement has influenced your career path. Do you intend to pursue the career in which you took your work placement? Give one reason for your answer.

(j) Write a letter of thanks to your employer for providing you with the work placement. In the letter, outline two ways in which you benefited from the experience, and outline one way in which it will help you in the future.

(k) As part of your LCVP course you have undertaken work placement/work shadowing.

(i) List three advantages of doing work placement/work shadowing.

(ii) State and explain the steps involved in securing the work placement/work shadowing.

(iii) Explain three obligations that an employer has regarding Health and Safety at work. Explain two obligations that an employee has regarding Health and Safety at work.

(iv) Using three separate headings, write a brief evaluation of your work placement/work shadowing.

(2002 LCVP Examination)

LINK MODULE 2

ENTERPRISE EDUCATION

Business Environment

Teamwork

Leadership

5

Enterprise Skills

At the end of this chapter students should be able to (tick ✓ the box when completed):

* Describe the qualities and skills of enterprising people. ☐

* Recognise examples of personal, community and entrepreneurial enterprise. ☐

* Identify personal strengths and weaknesses. ☐

* Suggest a course of action appropriate to improving personal enterprise skills. ☐

* Work co-operatively with others as part of a team. ☐

* Appreciate the value of teamwork in generating ideas, assessing risks, solving problems and completing tasks. ☐

* Undertake leadership of a group in an appropriate activity. ☐

* Plan and organise a meeting. ☐

* Make a presentation to both peers and adults. ☐

* Link the activities in this unit to learning in relevant Leaving Certificate subjects. ☐

* Evaluate the successes achieved and problems encountered in this unit. ☐

Enterprise

Notes

Definition:

Enterprise is the act of doing something new and challenging, taking the initiative and being prepared to take the risk.

The risk associated with enterprise may be in the form of money, time, reputation, energy, career commitment etc. In LCVP, when we talk about enterprise we do so in a broad context:

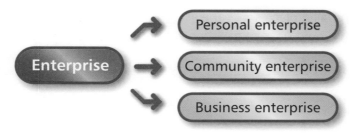

Personal enterprise
Examples of personal enterprise include undertaking a course to improve or acquire qualifications/skills, getting a part-time job, and organising activities in school or with friends.

Community enterprise
Community enterprise is when people get together on a voluntary basis to improve or promote their local area or simply to help others. Examples include local sports organisations, community council/centres, charity organisations and Tidy Towns' committees.

Business enterprise
An enterprising person who sets up a business to provide a good/service is called an **entrepreneur**. All enterprising people are not necessarily entrepreneurs, but entrepreneurs are enterprising people. Entrepreneurs are highly motivated hard-working people who take calculated risks in setting up businesses. Examples include Richard Branson, Louis Walsh, Tony Ryan, Tony O'Reilly, JP McManus, Harry Crosbie, Bill Gates and local business people in your own area.

Innate - Born with

Enterprise Qualities and Skills

Qualities are the characteristics that you are born with or develop as you grow up.

All enterprising people have some of the following qualities.
* Innovative (e.g. new ideas, new approaches, new methods etc.).
* Determined.
* Hard working.
* Ambitious.
* Realistic.
* Analytical (able to size up and understand situations quickly).
* Risk-taker.
* Self-confident.
* Flexible/adaptable.
* Decisive.
* Optimistic.

Task

(a) On your own, or in pairs, place **six** of the listed qualities that you think a successful enterprising person would possess in order of importance from 1 to 6.

1. _Determined_
2. _Ambicious_
3. _Optimistic_
4. _Risk-Taker_
5. _Realistic_
6. _Innovative._

(b) Identify any enterprising qualities that you believe you have.

1. _Optimistic_
2. _self-confident_
3. _Flexible_
4. _realistic_
5. _risk-taker_
6. _ambicious_

Skills describe those talents that you have acquired over time through training or practice. Enterprising people must develop a range of skills to help them to become dynamic motivated people who get things done.

Enterprising skills include the following.

* Planning skills (e.g. setting targets, etc.).
* Human relations skills (dealing well with others/getting on with people).
* Leadership skills (including motivating, delegating, etc.).
* Communication skills.
* Time management skills.
* Decision-making skills.
* Ability to deal with conflict.
* Creative/innovative skills.
* Ability to assess risks (risk taking).

> It can sometimes be difficult to distinguish between a quality and a skill, e.g. risk taker. However, do **not** use the same point as a skill and a quality.

Many of these skills are used together, e.g. communication skills as part of dealing with conflict, decision-making skills with planning, human relations skills with leadership skills, etc. Enterprising people may also possess other skills, e.g. practical skills such as computer skills, artistic skills, language skills, but these are not enterprise skills.

Task

(a) Identify any enterprising skills that you think you have. Feel free to add any enterprising skills that you believe should be on the list.

1. _Optimistic_   4. _realistic_

2. _self-confident_   5. _risk-taker_

3. _Flexible_   6. _ambicious_

(b) Identify other personal skills that you possess (see Chapter 3).

1. _Practical_   4. _____

2. _Interpersonal_   5. _____

3. _____   6. _____

(c) Are there any enterprise skills that you do **not** possess? Name **two**.

1. _Analytical_

2. _Decisive._

Websites
www.enterpriseboards.ie
www.lcvp.slss.ie
www.enterprise-ireland.com
www.irishentrepreneur.com
www.studententerprise.ie
www.forfas.ie
www.irc-ireland.ie
www.spiritofenterprise.net
www.skoool.ie

Teamwork

Teamwork involves working co-operatively with others in order to achieve the stated objectives. It is a major feature of working life today, and is a very important element of the LCVP.

There can be **five** stages in the life of a team:

Forming – when the team comes together for the first time.

Storming – when members compete for roles within the team and disagreements break out.

Norming – when members settle into their roles/responsibilities.

Performing – when the team performs together in order to achieve the objectives.

Mourning/transforming – when the team breaks up or a member leaves and a new team is formed.

The **benefits of teamwork** include the following.
* Sharing ideas, e.g. brainstorming.
* Sharing the workload.
* Decision-making – allows for consultation and problem solving.
* A range of experiences, skills and strengths among team members.
* Responsibility is shared – makes it easier to make difficult decisions.
* Work is completed faster.
* A sense of belonging improves motivation and morale.

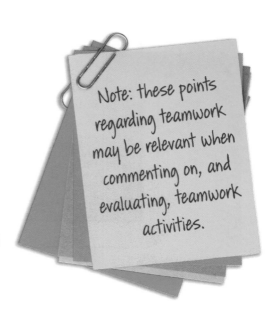

Note: these points regarding teamwork may be relevant when commenting on, and evaluating, teamwork activities.

In the LCVP, teamwork is a usual feature of the enterprise activity, where a group of students engage in a community or an entrepreneurial enterprise. Different teams may engage in different enterprises. Teamwork may also be a factor in a study of 'My Own Place', when organising a visit out, organising a visitor to the classroom, or investigating a local enterprise.

Some **difficulties** and/or **drawbacks** associated with teamwork include the following.

* Some members of the team may dominate.
* A team leader needs to be found and accepted by the other members.
* Training may be required before the team can work effectively.
* Planning and organising are required to coordinate the efforts of the team.
* Consultation can delay decision-making.
* Agreement may not be reached.
* Some members of the team may not 'pull their weight'. This can cause friction, as well as the failure to achieve the set targets.

Team members need to have the following **qualities** and **skills**.

* Willingness to cooperate.
* Flexibility.
* Sense of responsibility.
* Inter-personal skills.
* Ability to compromise.
* Listening skills.
* Leadership skills (team leader).
* Communication skills.

Leadership

Leadership has been defined as 'the process of influencing the activities of an organised group towards goal setting and goal accomplishment' (Reference: Stogdill). This definition of leadership means that everybody in certain circumstances may exercise leadership through their skills, expertise, knowledge or authority.

A leader needs to direct and coordinate the activities of the team in order to achieve the desired objectives.

Various studies have identified the qualities and skills associated with effective leaders. These include the following.

* Sense of responsibility.
* Concern for task completion.
* Energy/enthusiasm.
* Persistence/determination.
* Ability to assess and take risks.
* Originality/innovative.

* Self-confidence.
* Ability to handle stress.
* Ability to influence others.
* Capacity to coordinate the efforts of others.
* Communication skills.
* Ambition.

An effective leader will build on the strengths and talents of the people around him/her. He/she should be a good listener and a good communicator. A leader must also provide people with the necessary resources. He/she will allow others to take on responsibility and authority to work on their own initiative in order to achieve the agreed objectives. The leader also leads by example.

As part of LCVP activities involving teamwork, it is a good idea to give each student an opportunity to undertake a leadership role, in part or all of an activity. It is also important to acknowledge and encourage any exercise of leadership, e.g. leading by example or use of expert knowledge.

Task

(a) List three qualities of an effective leader, and give one reason why each quality is important.

(i) _____ (ii) _____ (iii) _____

Reasons:

(i) _____

(ii) _____

(iii) _____

(b) List three benefits and two drawbacks associated with working as part of a team within the LCVP.

Benefits:

(i) _____

(ii) _____

(iii) _____

Drawbacks:

(i) _____

(ii) _____

(c) Identify one financial risk and one non-financial risk facing an enterprising person, and explain each.

Financial risk: _____

_____

Non-financial risk: _____

_____

(d) Explain, with an example, the term 'initiative'.

_____

_____

Meetings

An essential part of teamwork, and leadership, is having regular meetings.

Preparing for a meeting

When **preparing for a meeting** a number of steps should be taken.

* Prepare an **agenda** for the meeting. The agenda is the list of topics to be discussed at the meeting.
* Send out a **notice of the meeting** and the agenda to all those entitled to attend the meeting. Give people adequate notice – usually a minimum of one week.
* Arrange a suitable **venue**.
* Ensure that the venue/room has adequate **facilities**, e.g. sufficient chairs, required equipment (e.g. data projector), adequate parking etc.
* Provide water for the speakers and/or for those attending. Light **refreshments** may also be provided on arrival or departure.

Running a meeting

In order to **run a meeting** efficiently, the following steps should also be taken.

* Appoint a chairperson (if you don't have one already).

Functions of a chairperson include the following.

* Run ('chair') the meeting.
* Ensure that order is maintained.
* Give each person an opportunity to speak, but watch the time.
* Organise a vote, if needed (may have a casting vote).
* Follow the order of the agenda.
* Represent the meeting/organisation.

* Keep to the agenda. Additional topics may be raised under 'A.O.B.' (Any Other Business) if this is on the agenda, or can be put on the agenda for the next meeting.
* Appoint a secretary (if none is in place) to keep a record of the meeting. This record is called the '**minutes**', and is a summary of what took place at the meeting and the decisions made.

Functions of the secretary include the following.

* Keep minutes of the meeting.
* Send out the agenda.
* Keep a register of members.

* Deal with all correspondence (send and receive letters etc.).
* Keep all official documents.

---

* Give each person an opportunity to speak on a topic, but set a time limit.
* If a motion is to be voted upon, then this should be properly organised according to the rules of the organisation, e.g. show of hands etc.
* Meetings are a waste of time if nothing is decided. Therefore, decisions need to be made and then implemented. Reading the minutes of the meeting at the **next** meeting allows feedback on implementation.

The following are examples of the notice, agenda and minutes of a meeting.

Notice and agenda

The treasurer is responsible for minding the money of the organisation. He/she must keep accurate accounts and report back to the group.

Notice and Agenda of the Meeting of the LCVP Fundraising Group

NOTICE

The meeting of the above group will take place in Room 4 on Wednesday 12 October 2011 at 1.15pm.

AGENDA

1. Minutes of the last meeting.
2. Matters arising from the minutes.
3. Correspondence.
4. Treasurer's report.
5. Fundraising ideas.
6. Organising team tasks.
7. A.O.B.

Signed: *P. McCormack*

Secretary

Minutes

Minutes of the Meeting of the LCVP Fundraising Group

The meeting of the above group took place in Room 4 on Wednesday 12 October at 1.15pm. A total of 16 attended.

1. The minutes from the last meeting were read out.
2. There were no matters arising from the minutes.
3. A letter was received from a local charity organisation thanking the group for the offer of fundraising. The charity has offered the services of a guest speaker. It was decided to invite the speaker to attend an LCVP class at a mutually acceptable time.
4. The treasurer reported that no funds have been raised to date.
5. A number of fundraising ideas were suggested and the group finally decided on investigating:
   (a) a sponsored 10km walk; and (b) a Christmas calendar with adverts.
6. Two teams of eight people were chosen to investigate each option, draw up a plan and report back at the next meeting. Each team will meet separately to assign duties.
7. There was no other business, so the meeting ended at 1.45pm.

The next meeting will take place on Wednesday 26 October 2011 at 1.15pm in Room 4.

Signed: *P. McCormack*

Secretary

> Note: each entry in the 'minutes' corresponds with the relevant entry in the 'agenda', and is an account of what took place at the meeting.

Task

Your LCVP class has been asked to get involved in an enterprise competition organised locally. Draw up an agenda for a class meeting to plan for and organise the competition. Your agenda should contain a minimum of **six** items.

Evaluation

Every activity in the LCVP involves
evaluation – see the Introduction section.

Evaluation

LCVP activity | Team performance | Own performance

Some questions to ask when evaluating an activity are as follows.
* Were the goals achieved?
* What did or did not work?
* What was learned from the activity?
* What problems were encountered and how were they dealt with?
* Was the activity worthwhile and/or cost-effective?
* How well did the team work together?
* How well did you perform your own role?
* What lessons can be learned for the future? Recommendations.
* What changes are needed to ensure success in other activities?

These are also the reasons for evaluation.

Conclusions

Recommendations

Recommendations must always be based on the conclusions.

Methods of Evaluation

An activity can be evaluated by methods such as the following.
* Comparing the objectives with the outcomes, in order to see what was achieved.
* Self-evaluation, where you reflect on the activity and your personal performance. This will eventually take the form of a written portfolio item, e.g. summary report.
* Group or class discussion, following completion of the activity.
* Feedback from the LCVP teacher(s).
* Feedback from interviewing other parties, e.g. speakers and customers.
* Using a questionnaire – a list of questions designed to obtain feedback and opinions from the various parties involved in the activity.

Task

(a) Why is evaluation important? Give three reasons for your answer.

(i) _____

_____

(ii) _____

_____

(iii) _____

_____

(b) Outline two ways in which an LCVP class enterprise could be evaluated.

(i) _____

_____

(ii) _____

_____

Making a Presentation

'A presentation involves the preparation and delivery of essential subject matter in a logical, condensed form, leading to productive results' (Reference: Morrisey, Sechrest, & Warman).

When making an effective presentation, the following factors should be taken into account.

* Establish your objectives. What are you trying to achieve with the presentation?
* Know your audience. This will affect your use of language, technical terms, the need for background information etc.
* Draw up a plan for your presentation – a beginning, a middle and an end. Remember your objectives. Remember 'ABC' – keep the information **a**ccurate, **b**rief and **c**lear.
* Prepare and organise any resource materials that you may wish to use. Ensure that the resource materials are relevant.
* If possible, make use of visual information – e.g. overheads, charts, powerpoint presentation – to reinforce the points being made.
* Ensure that the venue has all the facilities in place for your presentation.
* Use a variety of tone and gesture, speak clearly, use examples and summarise your points in order to get your message across.

In their book *'Loud and Clear – How to prepare and deliver effective business and technical presentations'*, Morrisey, Sechrest and Warman state the following.

'Your presentation is organised into three parts:
1. **Your opening** sells your audience on listening to your presentation, introduces the subject, and establishes your personal credibility.
2. **Your main content** makes up the bulk of your presentation and provides the detail necessary for your audience to understand your message.
3. **Your closing** allows you to summarise your main ideas, review the purpose of your presentation, and appeal for audience action.'

Remember: if you are intending to submit a recorded presentation as part of your LCVP portfolio, then you must include a question and answer session, as the candidate will be marked on his/her ability to elaborate on points and questions, and his/her ability to express opinions.

No two portfolio items can be on the same LCVP activity – excluding the Plan and Formal Report.

Task

(a) What Leaving Certificate subjects are, in your opinion, relevant to the following tasks and why?

   (i)   Organising or chairing a meeting: _____

   _____

   (ii) Organising an LCVP business enterprise: _____

   _____

   (iii) Making a presentation: _____

   _____

(b) Prepare a five-minute presentation to your class on an aspect of 'My Own Place' or on an investigation of a local enterprise/voluntary group. (This would not be suitable for the 'Recorded Interview/Presentation' portfolio item without incorporating a question and answer format.)

(c) List, and explain, two skills that you believe are needed to chair a meeting.

   (i)   _____

   _____

   (ii) _____

   _____

List two skills that you believe are needed to be a club secretary. Give a reason for each choice.

(i) _____

_____

(ii) _____

_____

(d) Write four questions that could be used in evaluating an activity?

(i) _____

(ii) _____

(iii) _____

(iv) _____

(e) Name two voluntary bodies that carry out community work in your area. Select one of the bodies mentioned and draw up an agenda for a monthly meeting.
(2003 LCVP Examination)

(f) Research has indicated that successful people are good communicators.
(i) Describe what is meant by the term 'good communicator'.
(ii) Outline three ways of improving your communication skills.
(iii) State and explain three personal characteristics of a successful entrepreneur.
(iv) Describe in detail three reasons why a business might fail.
(2002 LCVP Examination)

(g) Your class is planning to visit a local enterprise and you have been asked to organise a meeting to plan the visit.
(i) List three steps that you should take to organise the meeting.
(ii) Draw up an agenda for the meeting.
(iii) Identify three objectives the LCVP class might have for the visit.
(iv) Briefly describe two ways in which a local enterprise can benefit a local community.
(v) Write up a brief account (minutes) of the meeting.
(vi) Your classmates have been asked to evaluate your organisation of the meeting. Describe one method of evaluation and name two aspects that they should comment on.

6

Local Business Enterprises

At the end of this chapter students should be able to (tick ✓ the box when completed):

* Identify a range of enterprises in the local community. ☐

* Understand how an enterprise starts up and what support/training is available. ☐

* Describe the steps required to plan and carry out an investigation of a local enterprise. ☐

* Use learning from relevant Leaving Certificate subjects to formulate questions about aspects of a local enterprise. ☐

* Organise a visit to a local enterprise and invite appropriate speakers to visit the group in school. ☐

* Carry out a SWOT analysis of a business. ☐

* Report accurately on both a visit by an entrepreneur to a classroom and on a class visit to a local enterprise. ☐

* Compare and contrast information gathered on a group visit to a local enterprise. ☐

* Describe a local enterprise with particular reference to products, services, markets and workforce. ☐

* Understand and describe the different roles of adults working in a business environment. ☐

* Describe the impact of the Single European Market on a specific enterprise. ☐

* Describe and evaluate the use of information and communication technologies in a business enterprise. ☐

* Understand the importance of education and training in the development of a business enterprise. ☐

* Link the activities in this chapter to learning in relevant Leaving Certificate subjects. ☐

* Evaluate the successes achieved and problems encountered in this chapter. ☐

Local Enterprises

In Chapter 1, the three main types of economic activity in your local area were identified:
* Primary.
* Secondary.
* Tertiary.

Task

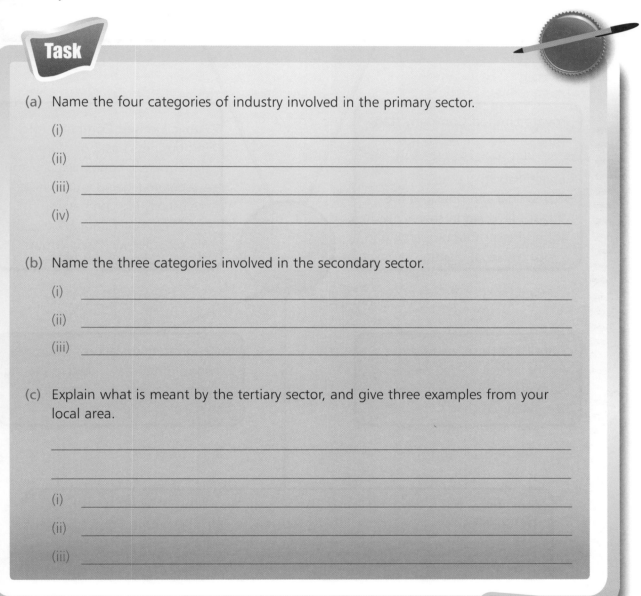

(a) Name the four categories of industry involved in the primary sector.

   (i) _____

   (ii) _____

   (iii) _____

   (iv) _____

(b) Name the three categories involved in the secondary sector.

   (i) _____

   (ii) _____

   (iii) _____

(c) Explain what is meant by the tertiary sector, and give three examples from your local area.

   _____

   _____

   (i) _____

   (ii) _____

   (iii) _____

Now we are going to categorise local enterprises under the type/form of business ownership. The main types of business ownership are as follows:

Sole trader – a business owned by one person, e.g. newsagent.

Partnership – a business owned by 2–20 partners who share the ownership, responsibility and the profit/loss.

Private Limited Company (Ltd) – the private limited company has 1–50 shareholders, with limited liability (i.e. the shareholder can only lose the amount invested in shares and not his/her private property) and a separate legal identity.

Public Limited Company (plc) – this business has 7 or more shareholders, limited liability and a separate legal identity. These are usually big companies, including multinationals, e.g. AIB plc, CRH plc, Kerry Group.

Types of Business

State Enterprise – a business and/or service owned by the State, e.g. ESB, Bord na Mona, IDA Ireland.

A Co-operative – a local enterprise comprising at least 7 people sharing a common bond, e.g. credit union, and having limited liability.

Franchise – this is were a business operates under a 'licence' from a franchisor, e.g. Supermacs, McDonald's, Subway. There is a legal and business arrangement in place, and the business (franchisee) pays a fee and a percentage (%) of the profit. (Usually operates as a private limited company.)

There are also community and voluntary enterprises in your area; however, in this chapter we are concerned with 'local business enterprises'.

Business enterprises can also be classified according to the size of the workforce: small (0–50 employees), medium (51–250 employees) and large (over 251 employees).

Task

Insert the names of local business enterprises in the following table.

Sole Trader	Partnership	Private company	Public company	Co-operative	State Enterprise	Franchise

Enterprise Start-up and Support

There are many different types of enterprises and therefore a lot of different ways for these enterprises to start up and/or develop. However, all of these enterprises share certain common start-up considerations.

What product or service is your business going to provide?

This involves generating the idea for the product/service, developing the concept, carrying out a feasibility study, undertaking product testing, and finally producing the product or service. It is essential that the enterprise also undertakes **market research** as part of this process. Is there a gap in the market? Is there a market in the gap? (We will examine all of this in more detail in Chapter 8.)

The need for finance

The enterprise will need to raise sufficient funds to obtain premises, equipment, hire staff, purchase stock etc. Finance can be raised from a variety of sources including the following.

* Savings.
* Redundancy money.
* Loans/investment from friends and relations.
* Set up the enterprise with a partner.
* Grants, e.g. local enterprise board, IDA Ireland, Forbairt.
* Loans from banks, e.g. term loans, bank overdraft.
* Sell shares. Companies and co-operatives can sell shares to interested investors (shareholders), who in turn get a vote in the enterprise and a share of the profit (dividend).

Task

Ask a Business teacher about other sources of finance for a business, and about how the sources are divided into short term (less than 1 year), medium term (1–3 years) and long term (over 5 years). Name three more sources of finance for a business enterprise.

(i) _____

(ii) _____

(iii) _____

What type of business organisation should you set up?

Will you set up as a sole trader, a company or some other option?

Where will you locate your business?

This is very important as you must consider being accessible to your customers, access to raw materials, available services, proximity to different methods of transport, cost of location etc.

The need to recruit and train staff

Refer back to Link Module 1.

The need to develop a suitable 'marketing mix' for the enterprise's product/service

The marketing mix is a combination of four factors that encourage the sale of the enterprise's product/service. The four factors are **Product**, **Price**, **Promotion** and **Place** (known as the **4Ps**). (Further information on the 4Ps can be found in Chapter 8.)

Ideally, a product/service should have a unique selling point (USP), a well known name (brand name), be reasonably priced, promoted using suitable media, and targeted and distributed to a chosen market ('target market').

Advice, finance, support and/or training are available from a wide variety of sources when starting up an enterprise. These include the following.

* Banks – sources of finance, advice etc.
* Enterprise Boards – set up to give advice, support and grants to local commercial enterprises (with employment potential up to 10 people), e.g. Limerick City Enterprise Board (www.limceb.ie). Feasibility study grants, employment grants and capital grants are available for suitable projects.
* Area Partnership Companies (see Chapter 1).
* LEADER – Partnerships (see Chapter 1).
* FÁS – training programmes for business start-up, staff training etc. (see Chapter 1).
* Other government agencies, e.g. Shannon Development, Teagasc, Bord Fáilte, Údarás na Gaeltachta.
* Project Development Centre, Docklands Innovation Park, 128–130 East Wall Road, Dublin 3.
* Small Firms Association, Confederation House, 84–86 Lower Baggot St, Dublin 2.

Websites
www.sfa.ie
www.udaras.ie
www.pdc.ie
www.failte.ie
www.shannon-dev.ie
www.dceb.ie

Investigation of a Local Enterprise

When investigating a local enterprise, the following steps are recommended.

(a) Divide into **teams** and assign each team to a specific local enterprise, or an aspect of the enterprise (e.g. marketing, management structure).
(b) Each team should set targets (**objectives**) to be achieved. For example, what do you want to learn about the enterprise, the skills you hope to learn/improve by carrying out an investigation (a personal objective) etc.
(c) Set a **time frame** for the investigation – a date by which each investigation must be complete.

(d) Try to choose an enterprise that has **relevance/interest** for you, e.g. cross-curricular appeal, career implications etc. This will allow you to ask for assistance from other teachers, e.g. Business, Career Guidance, Home Economics, Geography.

(e) Based on your objectives, formulate a set of **questions** to ask about different aspects of the enterprise.

> You will need to ask specific questions if you wish to receive specific information. Use other subject areas to help you to formulate relevant questions. Sample questions could include:
>
> * How many people are employed?
> * How do you recruit new employees?
> * What skills and qualities do you look for in employees?
> * What are the main health and safety features?
> * What type of business organisation is the enterprise?
>
> * Where, and to whom, do you sell your product/service?
> * What methods of advertising do you use and why?
> * Why did you choose the location?
> * Has the EU had any effects on the enterprise? If so, what are they?

(f) Decide on appropriate methods of **research**. For example, enterprise leaflets/brochures, Internet, library, visitor to the classroom, visit the enterprise, interview etc.

(g) Carry out the **investigation**.

(h) **Record** the findings.

(i) Draw **conclusions** based on the findings. Did you achieve your objectives? Was the activity a success or a failure?

(j) What recommendations, if any, would you make for future investigations?

(k) Finally, it is very important to **evaluate** the activity. What did you learn about the enterprise? What skills did you learn or improve? Did you enjoy/benefit from the activity?

> When evaluating an activity, you need to evaluate three things.
> * How did the activity itself go? Did we achieve the objectives set?
> * How did we perform as a team, i.e. the group activity?
> * How well did I do? Did I complete my task? (Personal evaluation.)
>
> Methods of evaluation include the following.
> * Self-evaluation.
> * Group discussion and evaluation.
> * Feedback from a teacher, speaker etc.
> * Giving a questionnaire to team members, the business enterprise etc.

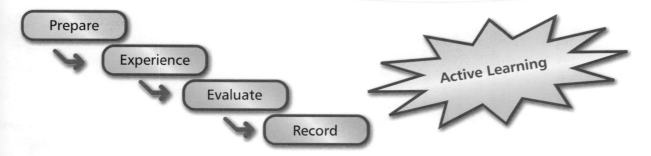

When analysing and/or describing a local enterprise, you could look at some, or all, of the following headings:

SWOT Analysis

When analysing an enterprise (or any organisation), with a view to assessing its position and planning for the future, it is recommended to carry out a **SWOT analysis**. SWOT stands for:

S = **Strengths**, i.e. strong points in the enterprise.

W = **Weaknesses**, i.e. areas of the enterprise that need to be developed.

O = **Opportunities**, i.e. what the future could potentially hold.

T = **Threats**, i.e. what possible dangers are lurking out there.

This can also be referred to as a SCOT analysis: Strengths, Challenges, Opportunities and Threats.

The **strengths** of an enterprise might include reputation (including trademark and brand name), dedicated workforce, skilled workforce, location, strong market share, value of assets etc.

The **weaknesses** (challenges) of an enterprise might include lack of finance, high staff turnover, lack of specialist staff members (e.g. language skills, computer skills), outdated assets, poor industrial relations etc.

The **opportunities** facing the enterprise might include a new market, increased market share, increased profits, new product range, employing more people, helping the public etc.

The possible **threats** facing an enterprise could include competition, loss of sales and customers, risk of closure/bankruptcy etc.

Note: you are expected to be able to complete a **SWOT analysis** in various activities throughout the LCVP course, e.g. the case study in the written examination, your enterprise activity, and analysis of a local business enterprise or local voluntary organisation.

Task

(a) Carry out a SWOT analysis of your school. Identify at least two strengths, two weaknesses, one opportunity and one threat.

(b) Carry out a SWOT analysis of a local enterprise. Identify two points under each of the four headings.

Organising a Visit Out/Visitor

Whether it is organising a visit out to a local enterprise, or a visitor (speaker) to come to the school, a number of steps should be followed.

* Contact the local organisation by telephone and/or by letter to arrange a suitable date and time for the visit.
* Obtain permission for the trip out or to have a speaker come into the school.
* Following discussions with all concerned, specify the objectives to be achieved by the visit/visitor.
* If organising a visit out, suitable transport and insurance cover must be organised and money collected. (Hint: organising the trip could be an enterprise for some people in the class.)
* Draw up a set of questions to ask during the visit. Questions could be allocated to different members of the class.
* If arranging for a visitor to come to the school, ensure that the room has adequate seating, the required equipment (such as a data projector, screen etc.) and water for the speaker(s). (It would also be nice to provide refreshments for the speakers before or after the talk.)
* Do research beforehand so that everyone is aware of the work/functions of the enterprise and the purpose of the visit.
* Give somebody the role of welcoming the visitor, and get another person to thank the visitor for their time and expertise. Follow a similar procedure if on a visit out to a local enterprise. Polite and proper behaviour is essential on all such occasions. Your own reputation, and that of the school, is affected.
* If visiting an enterprise, it is a good idea to divide the class into teams, with each team asked to specialise on some aspect of the enterprise, e.g. background, marketing etc.

* After the visit/visitor, it is a very important part of the LCVP to have a debriefing session. The purpose of the debriefing is to determine what people learned from the experience, whether it was worthwhile, to compare and share information gathered, and to evaluate the experience with reference to the initial objectives.

* Write a letter of thanks to the enterprise for their participation. This could be a specific task or role for a student.

* Students can now write up a Summary Report on the experience, including a personal evaluation of the experience. The student should include his/her specific role in the activity in his/her report. (See Chapter 1 or 'My Portfolio'.)

The visit out/visitor exercise, or the investigation of the local enterprise, could be the basis for the **Plan** (see Chapter 7 and 'My Portfolio'), or the **Presentation** (see Chapter 5 and 'My Portfolio'), or form part of the **'My Own Place' Report** (see Chapter 1 and 'My Portfolio'). However, **no two portfolio items can be on the same activity** – see the guidelines.

Websites
www.musgravegroup.com
www.supermacs.ie
www.centra.ie
www.kompass.ie
www.intel.ie
www.esso.ie
www.mace.ie
www.dunnesstores.ie
www.goldenpages.ie

 Task

(a) Imagine that a speaker from a local enterprise is due to visit your class to give a 30-minute presentation, including a question and answer session.
   (i) What steps should the class take to prepare for the visit?
   (ii) Prepare **six** questions that you could ask the visitor.

(b) Write a brief summary (200–300 words) of an enterprise from the above list of websites.

Role of Adults Working in a Business Environment

The role of adults in the workplace can be categorised in a number of different ways, including the following.

Skill

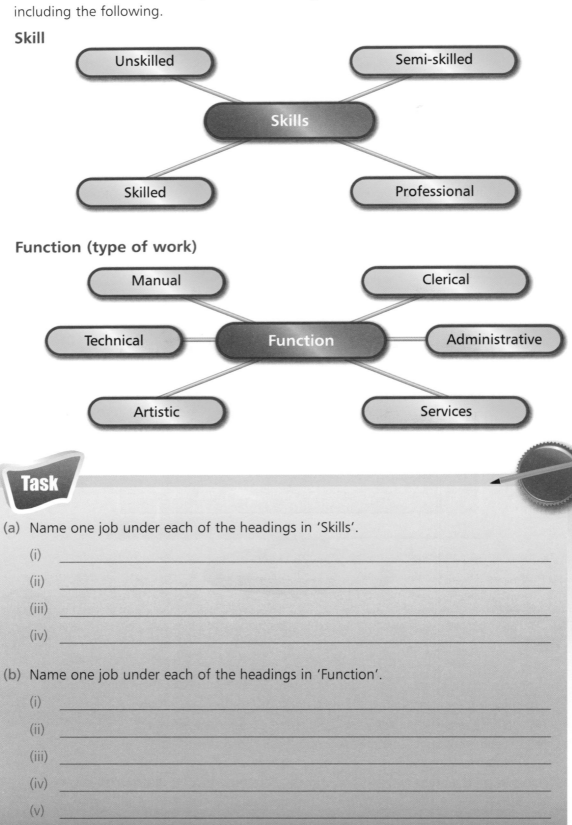

Function (type of work)

Task

(a) Name one job under each of the headings in 'Skills'.

(i) _____

(ii) _____

(iii) _____

(iv) _____

(b) Name one job under each of the headings in 'Function'.

(i) _____

(ii) _____

(iii) _____

(iv) _____

(v) _____

(vi) _____

Chain of command/organisation

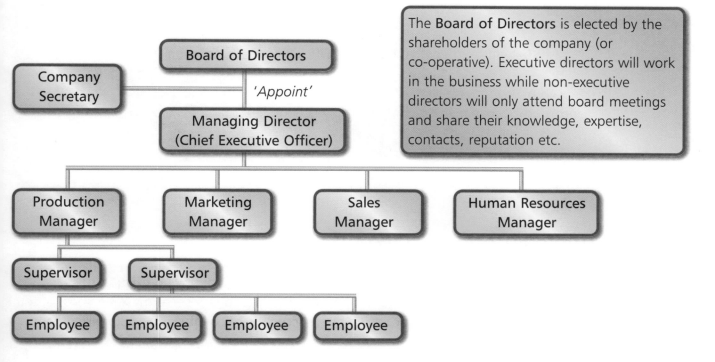

The **Board of Directors** is elected by the shareholders of the company (or co-operative). Executive directors will work in the business while non-executive directors will only attend board meetings and share their knowledge, expertise, contacts, reputation etc.

Note: The Board appoint a **Managing Director** (Chief Executive) to run the enterprise on a day-to-day basis according to the agreed business plan, and to report back. Each department has a manager in charge. He/she is responsible for the work of that department and for the targets being met. He/she delegates work and responsibility to assistant managers, supervisors and, in turn, to the workers.

Team members

Workers may also work as part of a team (see Chapter 5). Adults in the workplace should cooperate, share decision-making and share the workload. Teams will be given targets to achieve, and bonuses etc. will depend on the team performance and their ability to work together. There may also be a social aspect to teamwork, both inside and outside the workplace.

Some people in the workplace may also have specialist roles in addition to their normal job. These include the following.

❋ Health & Safety Officer.

❋ Shop Steward – the representative of the trade union elected by the workers in the trade union.

❋ Employee representative on the Board of Directors (semi-state bodies) or Board of Management (schools).

Task

(a) List two benefits and two drawbacks or difficulties associated with teamwork.

(b) Explain briefly the role of: (i) the Board of Directors; (ii) the Chief Executive Officer; and (iii) the Company Secretary. (You may need to ask a Business teacher for assistance.)

Single European Market (SEM)

'The single market is all about **bringing down barriers** and **simplifying existing rules** to enable everyone in the EU – individuals, consumers and businesses – to make the most of the opportunities offered to them by having direct access to 27 countries and 480 million people.

The cornerstones of the single market are often said to be the '**four freedoms**' – the free movement of **people, goods, services** and **capital**. These freedoms are enshrined in the EC Treaty and form the basis of the single market framework.'

(Source: http://ec.europa.eu/internal_market/)

The Single European Market (SEM) means that there are no barriers to the movement of goods, services, labour and capital throughout the EU member states. This has implications (both positive and negative) for Irish enterprises.

The **positive implications** include the following.

* The free movement of trade between the member states (no import duties or other restrictions) means that Irish firms can treat the EU as their market. Ireland's population is less than 1% of the population of the EU so access to a wider market can be vital.
* Increased sales should result in increased profits, business expansion, job security etc.
* The euro (€) has simplified and facilitated trade and travel between those member states that are currently members of the European Monetary Union.
* Businesses taking advantage of the larger markets experience economies of scale (e.g. savings as a result of bulk buying, spreading the cost of advertising etc.) and therefore cheaper production costs.
* The free movement of capital and labour between member states, e.g. mutual recognition of qualifications, has facilitated labour movement.
* Reduction of barriers, including simplification of trade documentation, similar regulations, product recognition etc., has reduced export costs and facilitated trade.

The **negative implications** include the following.

* More competition from EU businesses selling, and/or locating, in Ireland, e.g. Aldi.
* EU laws and regulations to bring goods/services up to standard may increase costs.
* A need for employees with language skills, if wishing to do business abroad.
* Increased risk of business failure as a result of increased competition, regulations etc.
* Cheaper labour costs, and other costs, in other EU member states may discourage businesses from locating in Ireland, resulting in possible job losses.

Task

Describe three effects that the SEM has had on a business that you are familiar with. Give details of the consequences it had for the business.

Information and Communication Technologies

The past 20 years or so has seen tremendous developments in, and the widespread use of, information and communication technologies, e.g. e-mail, mobile phones, Twitter, Skype etc.

These technologies have been used in business enterprises in a large number of ways including the following.

* Mobile phone technology, e.g. contacting sales people, working away from the office etc.
* Video-conferencing, allowing people to hold meetings with people from around the world without leaving the office, thus saving time and travel expenses.
* The Internet is used to research information (e.g. search engines such as www.google.ie) and to advertise on web pages, allowing global access, e.g. www.skype.com, www.ebay.ie.
* E-mail is used for sending messages, attaching documentation/photos etc.
* Electronic Data Interchange allows one computer to communicate with another automatically, e.g. automated stock ordering system when stock levels reach a predetermined minimum level.
* Computers with software packages for PowerPoint presentations, stock control systems (barcode), payroll management, personnel records etc.
* Workers can be facilitated to work from home, resulting in a reduction of costs (overheads).

* Forecasting model software, e.g. cash flow models, can assist in decision-making.
* Desktop publishing packages enable businesses to prepare brochures, leaflets, advertisements etc.
* Computer-based training facilitates the interactive training of employees.

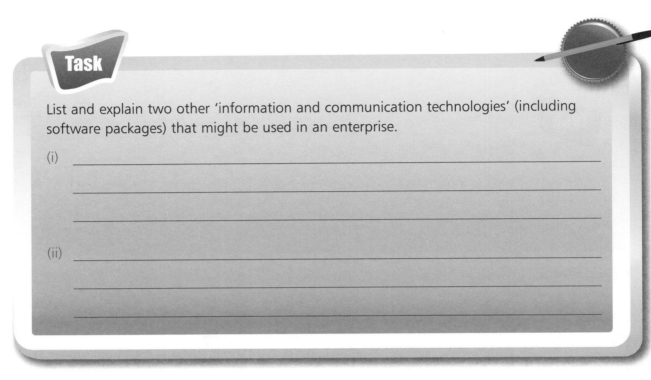

Task

List and explain two other 'information and communication technologies' (including software packages) that might be used in an enterprise.

(i) _____

_____

_____

(ii) _____

_____

_____

Importance of Education and Training

A wide range of knowledge and expertise is required when setting up an enterprise. The entrepreneur setting up the business needs to hire people with the skills and knowledge that he/she does not have, e.g. accountant, linguist, chemist etc. The entrepreneur will also need to understand what these skilled workers are doing and/or saying, as decisions will have to be made. Therefore, a certain level of intelligence, education and training is required.

In today's world, every entrepreneur needs a basic level of education (the more the better), must be determined and hard working (see enterprise qualities), and receive some level of training (even self-taught) and support, in order to ensure that the enterprise is an ongoing success. (Refer back to the sources of enterprise training and support.)

Task

(a) Describe a local business enterprise of your choice under the following headings:
(i) Products/Services; (ii) Workforce; (iii) Advertising; (iv) Market(s).

(i) _____

_____

_____

(ii) _____

_____

_____

(iii) _____

_____

_____

_____

(iv) _____

_____

_____

(b) Write a summary report (600 words or less) on **either** a visitor to your class or on a visit out to a local enterprise. Include an evaluation of how you believe that **you** benefited from this activity.

(c) Your LCVP class is planning a visit to an enterprise or to a voluntary organisation in your area.
(i) Write a letter to the contact person in the chosen organisation, asking for permission for the visit and a suitable date and time.
(ii) Describe four steps you should take in preparing for the visit.
(iii) Outline two reasons why your LCVP class would undertake this visit.

(d) Your LCVP team/group has been asked to organise a visit out to a local business enterprise.
(i) Draw up an agenda for the meeting of your team to plan the organisation of the visit.
(ii) List two benefits and two drawbacks of working as part of a team.
(iii) List six possible questions that could be asked during the visit which are relevant to the LCVP syllabus.
(iv) Explain two possible methods of evaluating the visit out. Give two reasons why evaluating the visit out is important.

(e) A group of friends from the LCVP class, including yourself, want to do something enterprising during the summer holidays and make some money.
   (i)   Identify three methods of generating ideas for an enterprise.
   (ii)   Apply a SWOT analysis to the main enterprise idea.
   (iii)   Identify two possible sources of advice and/or finance for your enterprise.
   (iv)   With regard to your team members, name two technical/practical skills, two personal skills/qualities, and two interpersonal/group skills that would benefit the team and improve the likelihood of success.

(f)   (i)   Describe briefly any local enterprise or organisation you have visited.
   (ii)   Outline two ways in which the EU has affected the enterprise/organisation.
   (iii)   Identify and explain two factors which, in your opinion, have contributed to the success (or failure) of the enterprise.
   (iv)   Identify five steps your LCVP class should take to ensure that the visit is successfully organised.

(g)   (i)   Your LCVP team have been asked to investigate a local enterprise. Set out four steps you would take to organise and complete this task.
   (ii)   Identify three ways of collecting information for your investigation.
   (iii)   Identify two uses of ICT within the local enterprise, and give one benefit of each use for the enterprise.
   (iv)   Name a government (statutory) organisation that provides a service in your area. Identify and explain three benefits this organisation brings to your area.
   (v)   Identify three headings you would use in an evaluation of your investigation. Explain the importance of each.

Local Voluntary Organisations/ Community Enterprises

At the end of this chapter students should be able to (tick ✓ the box when completed):

* Identify the voluntary bodies that carry out community work in the locality. ☐

* Describe the work carried out by a range of voluntary groups in the locality. ☐

* Understand and describe the different roles of adults working in voluntary community organisations. ☐

* Organise a visit to a local community enterprise and/or invite an appropriate speaker to visit the group in school. ☐

* Use learning from relevant Leaving Certificate subjects to formulate questions about aspects of a community enterprise. ☐

* Integrate information from a variety of sources to prepare a report, a plan or a presentation on an aspect of community development. ☐

* Link the activities in this chapter to learning in relevant Leaving Certificate subjects. ☐

* Evaluate the successes achieved and problems encountered in this chapter. ☐

Voluntary Bodies

There is a wide range of voluntary bodies carrying out work in local communities across Ireland. They may be trying to protect, promote or develop the local community, e.g. Neighbourhood Watch schemes, Tidy Town committees, local festival organisations, community enterprise groups, credit unions etc. Other groups may be trying to protect the less well-off or the elderly, e.g. the Society of St Vincent de Paul, senior citizen groups etc. Some voluntary bodies promote sports, e.g. GAA, FAI etc.

There are also a large number of other bodies involved in a variety of activities including health care, training, young people, tourism etc. These include the Irish Red Cross, the Order of Malta, the Scouts, the Girl Guides, An Óige, the Civil Defence etc.

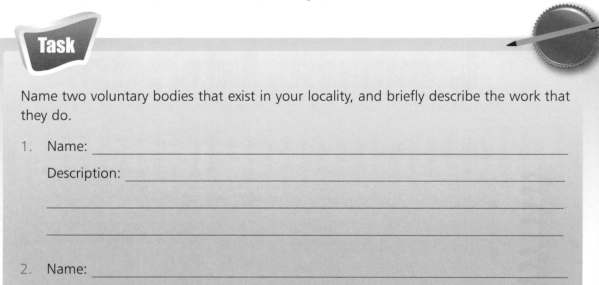

Task

Name two voluntary bodies that exist in your locality, and briefly describe the work that they do.

1. Name: _____

   Description: _____

   _____

   _____

2. Name: _____

   Description: _____

   _____

   _____

Websites

www.volunteer.ie   www.specialolympics.ie
www.trocaire.ie   www.svp.ie
www.volunteeringireland.ie   www.redcross.ie
www.scouts.ie   www.gaa.ie
www.ageaction.ie   www.creditunion.ie
www.irishgirlguides.ie   www.anoige.ie
www.cari.ie   www.civildefence.ie
www.cancer.ie

Task

Choose one of the above websites and describe, in 300–500 words, the work that the organisation does.

Impact of Voluntary Organisations on the Local Community

Community/voluntary organisations can benefit a local community in a number of ways, including the following.

* They provide a service that may otherwise not be available.
* They foster greater community spirit and involvement. This may result in other projects being undertaken.
* They can improve facilities and infrastructure in the locality, e.g. sports pitches, clubhouses, community centres etc. They may be able to obtain grants for community projects.
* They provide a good example to young people and may get them actively involved.
* They target those in need of a local service, e.g. the elderly, the young, the underprivileged, and attempt to meet their needs.
* By getting involved, they can give local people a sense of purpose and can improve organisational and planning skills, the ability to work as part of a team etc.

However, local community groups can suffer from difficulties such as lack of funds, a lack of experienced or skilled members, lack of facilities etc.

Role of Adults in Voluntary Organisations

In Chapter 6 we saw the different roles of adults in business enterprises. Adults may also have a number of different roles in voluntary community organisations. For example:

* Some adults are paid and work full- or part-time in the organisation, e.g. credit union personnel, senior GAA officials, etc. Most people give of their time for free (volunteer) and have a full-time job elsewhere.
* People can also be categorised by their role/job description when working in a voluntary organisation:

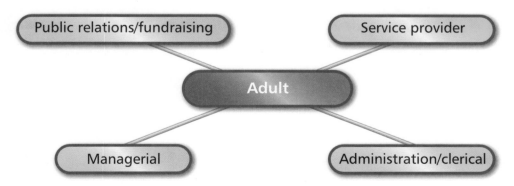

✳ People in voluntary organisations can also be divided into unskilled, semi-skilled and skilled workers, e.g. counsellors, coaches, paramedics, helpers etc.

Many people give of their time and energy selflessly and generously, and have often been volunteering for years.

Organising a Visit In/Visit Out

In Chapter 6 we looked at organising a visit into or out of the classroom. Look back and review the steps that need to be taken in order to organise such an activity. You will need to ask questions about the community enterprise. Here are some examples:

Hint: use your interests, Leaving Certificate subjects, and career path as the subject of questions. Also look at past examination questions.

✳ What services does the organisation provide?
✳ What skills/qualities do you need, if any, to become a member?
✳ What age must you be to join?
✳ How does being a member enhance your career opportunities?

Task

(a) Describe the steps that need to be taken in order to organise the visit in or the visit out.

(b) List six questions, other than those already given, that could be asked during the visit.

(c) Why is it important to evaluate the visit?

(d) Outline two methods of evaluating the visit.

Prepare a Report/Plan/Presentation

In Chapter 1 we looked at how to write a **Summary Report** outlining your main findings, and your conclusions, evaluation and recommendations based on these findings. You could now write a Summary Report based on the investigation of a local community organisation. Incorporate information learned from a visit out and/or a visitor, a website, an information brochure/leaflet etc. – see '**My Portfolio**'. (Note: information must **never** be copied into a report. This will result in marks being lost.)

You could also use the information gathered to make a **Presentation** (see Chapter 5) to your classmates and/or parents at an open night, or as the basis for your **Recorded Interview/Presentation** option in the LCVP portfolio.

Recorded Interview/Presentation

When Making a Presentation:

– Establish your objectives.
– Know your audience.
– Draw up a plan for your presentation – a beginning, a middle and an end.
– Remember 'abc' – keep the information accurate, brief and clear.
– Prepare and organise any resource materials that you may wish to use.
– If possible, make use of visual information, e.g. overhead slides.
– Ensure that the venue has the facilities you need.
– Use a variety of tone and gesture, and speak clearly.

During the Interview:

– Maintain eye contact with the person asking the question.
– Listen carefully to the question and answer each part.
– Sit upright and do not fidget. Body language is important.
– If you do not know the answer to a question, admit it rather than bluffing.
– Relax and be confident – you will be if you have prepared well.
– Be polite and thank the interviewer(s).

Interview Marking Scheme:

– Presentation, e.g. neatness. (0–4 marks).
– Variety of tone, gesture, diction, eye contact. (0–4 marks).
– Ability to communicate clearly, engage the audience, elaborate on points/questions, a logical sequence of thought (including the ability to express ideas and opinions clearly and knowledgeably). (0–36 marks)
– Information (content). (0–6 marks).

Remember: if you are intending to submit a recorded presentation as part of your LCVP portfolio, then you should include a question and answer session, as you will be marked on your ability to elaborate on points and questions, and your ability to express opinions.

No two portfolio items can be on the same LCVP activity – excluding the plan.

Alternatively, you could draw up a **plan** for carrying out an investigation of a local community group/organisation and use this as a **core portfolio item**.

Planning is an essential step in the learning cycle:

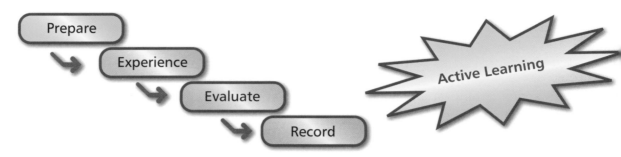

Prepare → Experience → Evaluate → Record

Active Learning

In fact, having a plan is very important in many different situations in everyday life, e.g. holiday plans, study plans, a budget (i.e. a plan of income and expenses) etc.

A **plan** sets out the target(s) to be achieved, and the course of action to be followed, in order for an activity to be achieved. Therefore, the plan should be in the **future tense** (see Portfolio Guidelines on page 124). It should also indicate some methods of how to evaluate the success of the activity when completed and if the objectives will have been achieved.

When planning an investigation of a local community enterprise (or a business enterprise), you should draw up a plan using the following suggested layout.

Note: In the section 'My Portfolio', there is a blank template on page 136 into which you can write your Plan, in preparation for typing the final version.

Plan of _____

Team Members:

Aim:

Objectives:

> The overall purpose.

> You should have 2-3 objectives. One objective should be a personal objective.

Research Methods:
What research methods will you use to research the organisation (activity), e.g. Internet, questionnaire, telephone, speaker, advice/guidance from adults or peers, etc? (I would recommend three research methods.)

> In a group activity, each student should also indicate the specific research he/she will carry out.

Analysis of Research:
Why have you chosen these research methods? Justify each method. Outline the information already obtained, or likely to be obtained, and how it will influence the plan.

SMART Plan:
– Specific
– Measurable
– Agreed
– Realistic
– Time frame

Page 1

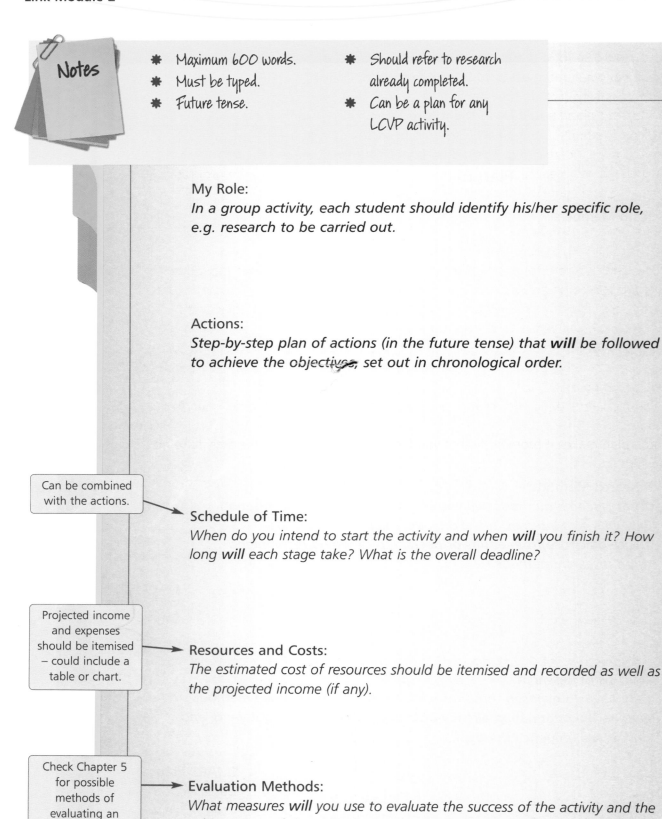

Notes

* Maximum 600 words.
* Must be typed.
* Future tense.
* Should refer to research already completed.
* Can be a plan for any LCVP activity.

My Role:
In a group activity, each student should identify his/her specific role, e.g. research to be carried out.

Actions:
*Step-by-step plan of actions (in the future tense) that **will** be followed to achieve the objectives, set out in chronological order.*

Can be combined with the actions.

Schedule of Time:
*When do you intend to start the activity and when **will** you finish it? How long **will** each stage take? What is the overall deadline?*

Projected income and expenses should be itemised – could include a table or chart.

Resources and Costs:
The estimated cost of resources should be itemised and recorded as well as the projected income (if any).

Check Chapter 5 for possible methods of evaluating an activity.

Evaluation Methods:
*What measures **will** you use to evaluate the success of the activity and the achievement of the objectives? You must refer to the stated objectives, including your personal objective (especially in a group activity).*

Page 2

Notes on the plan

✱ The plan could be for a group activity. However, each student must complete his/her own original plan, and must include **one** personal objective.

✱ In a group activity, include the heading 'My Role'.

✱ **Page 2 of the plan should be in the future tense.**

✱ 'Evaluation Methods': each objective should be referred to, and how you propose to measure if it will be achieved. The methods will need to measure whether the objectives will have been achieved in the time frame, and how you will measure the group (team) performance and your own personal performance.

Advantages of planning

The benefits of planning include the following.

✱ Objectives (targets) are set and agreed upon. The outcomes can then be measured against the agreed objectives.

✱ Everybody should be working together in order to achieve the agreed objectives. Everybody knows what has to be done and their role.

✱ Research should be carried out in advance so that there is a greater likelihood of success.

✱ Planning identifies in advance the resources (e.g. money, labour) that will be needed for the activity to be a success.

✱ The plan highlights difficulties **before** they actually occur, so steps can be taken to overcome any problems.

✱ Having a plan makes it more likely that you will receive approval for the activity to go ahead.

✱ The plan sets a time frame for the activity to be completed and the objectives to be achieved.

FAIL TO PREPARE, PREPARE TO FAIL.

Task

(a) Write out a **plan** for an investigation of a local community organisation that you, or your team, are about to undertake.

(b) Choose any three of your Leaving Certificate subjects. State how each subject could help you with an investigation of a local voluntary organisation.

(c) With reference to an investigation of a local voluntary organisation, or a visit in/visit out activity, outline any problems/difficulties that were encountered, how these were overcome and how successful you feel the activity was.

(d) In your opinion, how important is it to (i) plan and (ii) evaluate an activity? Give **two** reasons for each.

(e) Write a brief description of a local voluntary organisation (400 words).

(f) Write a letter (using today's date) inviting a representative of a local community organisation to visit your LCVP class to talk about the organisation.

(g) Your LCVP class has been asked to visit a voluntary organisation in your area.
   (i) Identify five questions that could be asked when visiting a voluntary organisation that would be relevant for your LCVP course.
   (ii) Describe four steps the class should take in preparing for the visit.
   (iii) Write a report and evaluation of a visit out, or a visitor in, your class has participated in.

(h) As part of your summer holidays you are planning to give some time as a volunteer for a local voluntary organisation.
   (i) Identify two personal skills and two personal qualities that you could bring to a voluntary organisation.
   (ii) Outline three possible benefits to you as a result of volunteering.
   (iii) Briefly describe three benefits that a local voluntary organisation brings to the community.
   (iv) Write out an enterprise/action plan for your planned activity. Identify in your plan at least two objectives.

(i) The people in your locality have joined together to form a community association.
   (i) List three benefits to an area of having a community association.
   (ii) List two 'threats'/difficulties facing most community associations.
   (iii) Name one successful voluntary organisation in your area.
   (iv) Outline the work of this organisation, indicating who benefits from it.
   (v) Complete a SWOT analysis of this organisation, giving at least one point under each heading.
   (vi) Local businesses frequently support local voluntary organisations. Why do you think they do this?
   (vii) Describe briefly two ways that local businesses can support local voluntary organisations.

(j) (i) Outline five steps that your LCVP class would need to take in order to organise and complete an investigation of a local voluntary organisation/local enterprise.
   (ii) Identify four reasons why planning the investigation in advance is so important.
   (iii) Give three reasons why it is essential to evaluate your investigation when completed. Name four headings you would use for this evaluation. Explain the importance of each.
   (iv) Prepare a five-minute presentation about the local voluntary organisation, including the objectives and scope of the investigation, and your findings.

8

An Enterprise Activity

At the end of this chapter students should be able to (tick ✓ the box when completed):

* Work co-operatively with others to generate a range of ideas. ☐

* Prepare a plan for the selected enterprise activity. ☐

* Identify available resources to support an enterprise activity. ☐

* Integrate information from a variety of sources including relevant Leaving Certificate subjects. ☐

* Assess personal and group skills and identify possible training needs. ☐

* Identify and recruit consultants willing to advise on a selected enterprise activity. ☐

* Understand the practical importance of market research and marketing mix. ☐

* Be aware of the concepts of publicity and promotion. ☐

* Actively participate in group work in a variety of roles – owner, worker, team leader. ☐

* Take responsibility to ensure that targets are reached. ☐

* Participate in a review of group performance. ☐

* Review personal performance in an enterprise activity. ☐

* Prepare and present a written or verbal report on an enterprise report. ☐

* Link the activities in this chapter to learning in relevant Leaving Certificate subjects. ☐

* Evaluate the successes achieved and problems encountered in this chapter. ☐

In the LCVP 'Link Modules', when dealing with enterprise, we distinguish between the following:

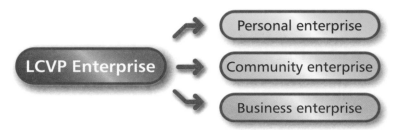

Your LCVP enterprise can be in **any** of these three areas.

Generating Ideas

When developing a product or service, a number of stages need to be completed. These can include the following.

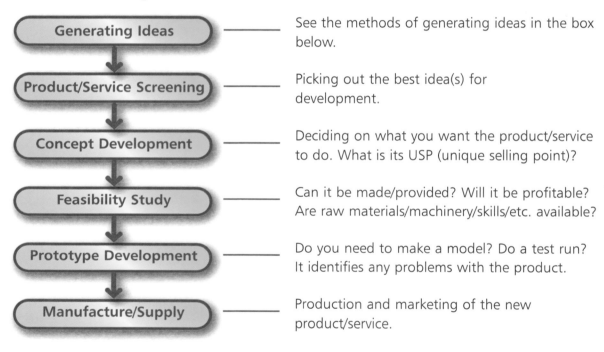

Generating Ideas	See the methods of generating ideas in the box below.
Product/Service Screening	Picking out the best idea(s) for development.
Concept Development	Deciding on what you want the product/service to do. What is its USP (unique selling point)?
Feasibility Study	Can it be made/provided? Will it be profitable? Are raw materials/machinery/skills/etc. available?
Prototype Development	Do you need to make a model? Do a test run? It identifies any problems with the product.
Manufacture/Supply	Production and marketing of the new product/service.

Ideas for a product(s) or service(s) can come from a variety of sources. These include the following.

* Copy existing products/services that are available, either at home or abroad.
* Improve on existing products/services.
* Identify a gap in the market where no suitable product/service exists.
* Suggestions from employees or customers, e.g. suggestion boxes.
* Research and development (R&D) within the business might generate ideas.
* 'Brainstorming' – when a group of people, sharing a common objective, expertise and knowledge, come together to generate ideas.

Task

(a) On your own, or in small groups, generate three ideas for LCVP enterprises that would be feasible for you and/or your class.

(i) _____

(ii) _____

(iii) _____

(b) Examine each of the three ideas and give one possible benefit and one possible drawback or difficulty for each.

(i) Benefit: _____

Drawback: _____

(ii) Benefit: _____

Drawback: _____

(iii) Benefit: _____

Drawback: _____

Enterprise Plan

The layout for a **plan** is shown in Chapter 7 as it should appear as a core LCVP portfolio item. You should use this layout again when drawing up the plan for your LCVP enterprise.

There are many important aspects to having a plan for an enterprise activity, including the following.

* Sets objectives (targets) that are to be achieved, and these are agreed upon.
* Identifies resources, e.g. money, labour etc., that will be needed.
* Identifies suitable methods of researching the enterprise and why you have chosen each method. Research should be carried out in advance so that there is a greater likelihood of success.
* Highlights any difficulties that are likely to arise so that you can take steps to eliminate them before they occur.
* Gives each member of the team a role to play in the enterprise.
* Will hopefully encourage investors to part with their money and also make it easier to gain permission for the enterprise within school.

> When you have the idea, draft the first part of the plan, do the research, and then see where that will take you with the rest of the plan.

* Focuses attention on how you propose to evaluate the success of the enterprise, and the evaluation methods that you intend to use, e.g. questionnaire.
* Sets a time frame for the activity to be completed and the objectives to be achieved.
* Can be used on an ongoing basis during the enterprise so that you do not stray too far from the plan.

Task

Draw up a **plan** for an enterprise activity of your choice. In the plan, identify three research methods that you intend to use.

Business Plan

When starting up in business, every aspiring entrepreneur is encouraged to draft a business plan. Advice and encouragement are available from organisations such as the enterprise boards, LEADER partnerships, Shannon Development, banks and so on.

In business, a **business plan** is an essential tool that does the following.
* Sets targets to be achieved.
* Describes the market research undertaken, and the results thereof.
* Describes the strategies that will be used to achieve the various targets.
* Gives information on the marketing mix – Product, Price, Place and Promotion (4Ps).
* Provides background information about the enterprise, e.g. the history of the business, the management team etc.
* Identifies the resources at the disposal of the business, including cash flow forecasts.

The **layout of a business plan** will usually include the following sections.

* **Summary** – the main points of the plan highlighting the objectives and proposed strategies.
* **History of the business** – this will include details of the setting up of the business, the type of business ownership, details of the owners, set-up capital, location etc.
* **Product/Service details** – details of the product, unique selling point (USP) etc.
* **Analysis of the market** – details of market research undertaken including customer preferences, location of the market, characteristics of the market etc.
* **Strategies** – including the marketing strategy (4Ps of Product, Price, Place and Promotion), sales forecasts etc.
* **Production details** – including details of the methods of production, the sources of raw materials, machinery requirements.

✱ **Management** – this may include the management structure and details of the senior management positions.

✱ **Financial plan** – this should include profit & loss accounts and balance sheets (actual and projected), projected cash flow forecasts, break-even charts, business ratios etc.

The **benefits** of having a business plan include the following.

✱ It highlights any difficulties and shortcomings **before** they actually occur.

✱ It lets everybody know what has to be done and their role and functions.

✱ It identifies the resources available and the resources that will be needed.

✱ It helps to keep the business focused, and the outcomes can be measured against the objectives.

✱ It persuades investors (including banks) to invest money in or lend money to the enterprise.

Websites
www.myownbusiness.org
http://articles.bplans.com
www.entrepreneur.com/businessplan/index.html
www.performanceplus.ireland.ie
www.bankofireland.ie/html/gws/business/
    start_your_own_business/

Task

You have started to work in a new business and have been asked to help develop the business plan for the new business for the coming year.

(i) Outline three reasons why it is important for a business/organisation to plan ahead.

(ii) Name one financial institution and one State organisation where the business may seek financial assistance. Outline the nature of this financial assistance in each case.

(iii) Describe three benefits of having a team of people working together to complete the plan.

(iv) Choose two sections from a business plan and describe each in detail.

Resources

When planning an enterprise, you should always examine the resources that you have at your disposal or that you might need. These include the following.

* **People resources** – includes each of the team members, their expertise, knowledge, contacts etc. It includes assistance from your LCVP teacher(s) and other subject teachers. Is assistance available from people outside of school (e.g. parents, employers, class visitors etc.)?

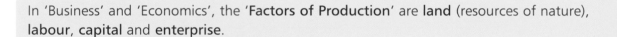

* **Financial resources** – how much money is available? Can you attract investors?
* **Assets** – what equipment is available? Do you have access to facilities?
* **Raw materials** – will raw materials be required? Are materials available to you within the school? Have you sourced and priced materials?
* **Enterprise** – have you and/or your team mates ideas for an enterprise? Are you prepared to work hard and take the necessary risks, e.g. risk of losing money, risk of failure?
* Use your other **Leaving Certificate subjects** to help in generating ideas and/or as the basis of your enterprise, e.g. an historical trail, a woodwork product, a cake sale etc.

In 'Business' and 'Economics', the '**Factors of Production**' are **land** (resources of nature), **labour**, **capital** and **enterprise**.

Now would be a good time to assess your personal skills, qualities, strengths and weaknesses, in the light of selecting an enterprise activity and your role in the activity. You may also need to assess your teamwork skills and qualities, if working as part of a team – see Chapter 5. When working together as a team, the members can complement each other, share the workload and share skills, knowledge, decision-making etc.

Task

(a) List two personal skills and two personal qualities that you believe will be required for an **enterprise** activity.

Personal Enterprise Skills	Personal Enterprise Qualities
1. _____	1. _____
2. _____	2. _____

(b) List two personal skills and two personal qualities that you believe will be required for working as part of a **team**.

Personal Teamwork Skills

1. _____

2. _____

Personal Teamwork Qualities

1. _____

2. _____

By completing a skills analysis, individuals and/or group members can identify any shortcomings and the need for training. For example, there might not be a team member with any knowledge or expertise in marketing or accounts. Then you need to identify where the training and/or advice is available. For example, you could look for consultants and/or trainers in the following areas.

* The LCVP teachers might be able to assist or advise you.
* Leaving Certificate subject teachers will have specialist knowledge/advice.
* Parents and family members may have the necessary knowledge, skills or contacts.
* Friends may have expert knowledge in the required area.
* Contacts made through LCVP activities, e.g. work experience, could be contacted for advice/training. (Please ask your teacher for advice on this first, as these people are busy and you do not want to annoy them and lose their support.)
* Local business people might provide advice and/or training as part of their business dealings, e.g. DIY shop, quotation from a printer etc.
* Local training and advisory agencies, e.g. Enterprise Board.

When working together in a team, each member should be encouraged to be actively involved. Each team member should have a specific function to complete, e.g. advertising, managing finances etc.

No team member should continuously dominate proceedings, decision-making etc. It is a good idea to rotate roles within the team. For example, each member could act as team leader for one week at a time; a different member could be chairperson at the meeting for that week etc.

Marketing

Marketing involves all the stages in the selling of a good or service. It involves doing research, buying raw materials, producing and distributing goods, advertising and after-sales service.

Marketing is the management process responsible for identifying, anticipating and satisfying the needs of customers profitably.

An essential element of marketing is market research.

Market Research
Market research is the collection, recording and detailed examination of all the information relating to the transfer of goods or services from the producer to the consumer.

Market research is essential for a number of reasons.
* It identifies what the public wants so that you can then provide this product/service.
* As a result of identifying the public's preferences, it increases the likelihood of success and, therefore, increases profits.
* It reduces the risk of errors and other costly mistakes, e.g. production changes.
* It provides essential information, such as market details (e.g. size, gender, location, spending capability, age) which will make decision-making a lot easier and more effective, e.g. most suitable advertising method(s), price to charge etc.
* It identifies the strengths and weaknesses of existing products/services, allowing improvements to be made.
* It keeps a close eye on the competition – if they have new products, the price they charge etc.

The **methods of market research** can be divided as follows.

1. **Desk research** – this is where information is gathered by doing research on data already available within the organisation or from outside agencies. Sources include the Internet, telephone, existing records in the filing cabinet or computer, publications etc. The information gathered is known as 'secondary data'.

2. **Field research** – this is where you need to find out first-hand information relevant to your enterprise, e.g. people's likes/dislikes, price they are willing to pay etc. This is called 'primary data'. Field research usually involves face-to-face interviews, telephone interviews/ research, postal questionnaires etc.

When undertaking field research it is very important to design a questionnaire so that you can find out the information you require directly from the people in the market.

Questionnaire

The following guidelines should be followed when designing a questionnaire.

* Keep it simple and clear.
* Ask simple and specific questions, e.g. give people choices to make from a selection, or ask yes/no type questions.
* Avoid open-ended questions, if possible, e.g. what do you like about ...?
* Include control questions where you check previous answers, and thereby check the accuracy of the information.

Example of a Questionnaire

LCVP QUESTIONNAIRE

As part of an LCVP enterprise activity, my group is investigating the possibility of producing a 6th Year 'Year Book', as a memento of their last year in this school. We hope that you will take a few minutes to complete this questionnaire.
Please tick (✓) your choice:

1. Should this Year Book contain:
   6th Year photos only ☐   6th Year photos with captions ☐
   6th Year photos with stories, articles, etc. ☐
   6th Year photos, captions, & stories, articles, etc. ☐

2. If including stories, poems, and articles (sports achievements, interviews, etc.) should these be from:
   6th Year only ☐   The entire school ☐

3. Would you prefer the photos to be:
   Black & White ☐   Colour ☐   Don't mind ☐

4. What is the maximum amount you would be willing to pay for the Year Book?
   (You can tick [✓] more than one box if you wish)

   €5-€6 ☐   €7-€8 ☐   €9-€10 ☐

5. Would you be interested in buying this Year Book?
   Yes ☐   No ☐

6. We intend to ask for a deposit (non-refundable) of €2 when accepting orders. Is this acceptable?
   Yes ☐   No ☐

7. What price would you consider to be too expensive for the Year Book and would be unwilling to pay?
   €7-€8 ☐   €9-€10 ☐   None ☐

8. What suggestions would you like to make concerning the Year Book and its layout/content?
   _____
   _____
   _____

Thank you for taking the time to complete this questionnaire. Please return it to one of the LCVP team members or to the box in the Secretary's Office marked 'LCVP Questionnaire'.

A questionnaire can then be distributed by post, by telephone or by a person-to-person interview (a likely option in a school situation).

Task

Design a one-page questionnaire for an LCVP group planning to sell 'hoodies' as their LCVP enterprise.

It is usually not possible to ask every one of your potential customers, i.e. your market, about the product or service; therefore, you have to decide who to ask. This can be done in a number of ways, including:

* **Random sample** – give the questionnaire to anyone.
* **Cluster sample** – give the questionnaire to people in a specific area.
* **Quota sample** – ask a specific group only, e.g. 6th Year students.

The information collected should then be recorded and analysed. The findings can be used to make important decisions, e.g. design, methods of promotion, price etc.

 ## The Marketing Mix

Every enterprise has to get four things right in order to successfully sell a product or service. These are known as the **4Ps**:

* Product.
* Price.
* Promotion.
* Place.

The objective is to have the right product at a suitable price in the right place using relevant promotion.

Product
* Find a gap in the market, satisfy customer needs and generate sales.
* Create an attractive and safe design for the product.
* Give the product a unique name, i.e. brand name (e.g. Pepsi).
* Use attractive and appropriate packaging (packaging also has to fulfil legal requirements).
* Have a USP (unique selling point) to attract potential customers, e.g. a unique function, an extensive after-sales service.
* Find out if there is competition.

Price
* The price must cover the direct costs (e.g. raw materials, labour).
* It must also cover marketing and distribution costs.
* It must take account of the competitor's price.
* The price must be in line with customer demand and what they are willing to pay.

Promotion
* What methods of **advertising** will you use to reach your target market, e.g. posters, newspaper?
* Will you give any **sales promotion** offers, e.g. 3 for the price of 2?
* Enterprises also have to deal with **public relations** issues, e.g. dealing with complaints, press releases etc.
* Will you employ **direct marketing**, e.g. a flyer or e-mail to each student?

Place
* Where is your market actually situated?
* How will you transport your goods to the market?
* How will you distribute your goods? Will you sell the goods direct to the customer or will you sell through an agent/retailer, e.g. school shop.

The 4Ps are covered in a lot more detail as part of the Business course. Perhaps a group of Business students could make a presentation to the class on the 4Ps, and/or on marketing in general.

Evaluation

On completion of an enterprise activity, all of the objectives should ideally be achieved, including any personal objective(s) that you set for yourself. It is the responsibility of every team member to ensure that the objectives are achieved and that they do not pass the blame onto somebody or something else, e.g. not enough time, not my job etc. In teamwork everybody should share the decision-making, the workload and the responsibility.

At the end of the enterprise activity, it is very important to evaluate the activity in order to do the following.
* **Highlight the successes and/or failures of the enterprise**. Were all of the objectives achieved? From your findings you can draw conclusions and make recommendations for future enterprises. The recommendations must be based on the conclusions and should highlight ways of avoiding problems and/or failures in the future.

* **Review group performance**, i.e. how people worked together. Did everybody play his/her part? Did any one person dominate? Were there serious disagreements? Were the team objectives achieved? Each team member should be given the opportunity to express his/her opinion, e.g. through a group discussion or a questionnaire. The team review could be part of any report or presentation.

* **Review personal performance**. How did you perform in the enterprise? Did you work well with others? Did you achieve your objectives? The personal review would also form an important part of the evaluation in any report or feedback.

* Identify if the activity was a **worthwhile experience** and what was learned from the activity.

The **methods of evaluation** can include the following.
* A group/class discussion.
* A questionnaire for team members and/or customers, speakers etc.
* Interviewing customers to obtain feedback.
* Feedback from the LCVP teacher(s).
* Measuring the achievement of objectives (e.g. money raised).
* Feedback from reports or personal accounts of the team members.
* Self-evaluation.

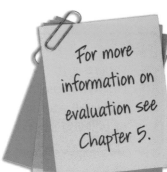

For more information on evaluation see Chapter 5.

Task

(a) Choose two methods of evaluating your LCVP activity/enterprise and give one reason for choosing each method.

(i) _____

Reason: _____

_____

_____

(ii) _____

Reason: _____

_____

_____

(b) Identify, and briefly explain, three areas of the enterprise/activity that need to be evaluated.

(i) _____

Explanation: _____

_____

_____

(ii) _____

Explanation: _____

_____

_____

(iii) _____

Explanation: _____

_____

_____

Enterprise Report

The **Enterprise Report** (and the 'My Own Place' Report) in the LCVP portfolio (both optional items) should be a word-processed document 1,000–1,500 words in length and must have page numbers. Both reports have very similar layouts. (Therefore, the Enterprise Report layout can be modified to use for the report on 'My Own Place'.)

> There are two formal reports as part of the portfolio:
> Enterprise/Activity Report.
> My Own Place Report (Chapter 1).
> See sections: Portfolio Guidelines and My Portfolio.

Suggested Layout (Guideline Only)

_____ REPORT

A Report on

_____

_____

Prepared by: _____

For the attention of: _____

Date: _____

Page 1

Title page

Table of Contents

Page 2

Table of Contents
Lists all of the headings and the pages that they are found on.

Summary

Terms of Reference

Aims & Objectives
*
*
*

Introduction

Page 3

The **Summary** should give a brief account of the enterprise and the main conclusions and recommendations.

The **Terms of Reference** are the instructions or guidelines given to the report writer.

The **Aims & Objectives** give the overall aim as well as the specific targets that are to be achieved. (Hint: look back at the Enterprise Plan.) At least one personal objective must be included.

The **Introduction** gives some background information, e.g. how the enterprise came about, team details etc.

(**Note:** in the 'My Own Place' Report, the Summary is not needed and the Introduction gives details on your local area, where the focus of the investigation will be, a map of the area etc.)

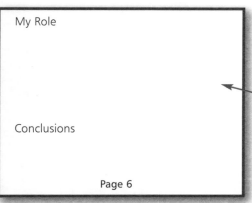

Planning
Research
Marketing
Page 4

Planning includes any issues to be dealt with, actions agreed, time frame etc.

Research gives details of any research undertaken, e.g. interviews, as part of the enterprise and the outcomes of the research.

Marketing refers to the marketing strategies undertaken in the enterprise (4Ps – Product, Price, Promotion and Place).

(**Note:** In the 'My Own Place' Report, replace the heading 'Marketing' with 'Out of School Activity', where you describe a 'field research' activity including the date of the activity, what took place, information gained etc.)

Organising the Event
The Actual Event
Page 5

Organising the Event – describes the activities leading up to the event, e.g. delegation of tasks, costs involved, facilities or resources required.

The **Actual Event** describes in detail the actual activity/enterprise. It should be written in a logical and chronological order. It should include at least two relevant illustrations, e.g. tables, charts.

(**Note:** In the 'My Own Place' Report, these heading are replaced by the headings 'Local Issue' and 'Findings', respectively. 'Local Issue' identifies and analyses an issue relevant to the area. 'Findings' are the outcomes of the investigation, including illustrations.)

My Role
Conclusions
Page 6

My Role: each student must identify his/her own personal contribution to the enterprise (investigation).

The **Conclusions** outline the outcomes of the enterprise, e.g. amount raised. The conclusions must relate to the body of the report and the stated aims and objectives.

Recommendations
Evaluation
Page 7

The **Recommendations** must be based on the report's conclusions and the carrying out of the enterprise/activity. They must make suggestions for future action.

The **Evaluation** should comprise the following.
* An evaluation of the enterprise/activity, e.g. were the objectives achieved?
* An evaluation of the group activity.
* Personal evaluation.

(The Conclusions & Recommendations can be presented in paragraph form or as bullet point lists.)

APPENDICES

Appendices are optional, and should be a maximum of two items. Appendices could include large illustrations (e.g. maps, tables, photos), financial data, diagrams, a copy of a questionnaire or advert etc.

When writing the report, you should adhere to the following guidelines.

* Have a clear and consistent layout.
* Be accurate, brief and clear.
* Present the information in a logical sequence, clearly and concisely.
* Communicate the information in appropriate detail.
* Use illustration(s) to support your findings.
* Draw conclusions and make recommendations appropriate to the body of the report.
* Evaluate the activity itself, the group performance and your personal contribution.
* Refer to other Leaving Certificate subjects that were relevant to the activity/enterprise.

 Attention must be paid **each year** to the guidelines issued by the State Examinations Commission regarding the LCVP portfolio and examination, as changes do take place.

 Task

(a) You are planning an enterprise of producing t-shirts with logos to sell within your school.
 (i) Describe two methods of research that you will need to carry out and give a reason for each.
 (ii) Design a questionnaire which you could give to fellow students in order to research your product.

(b) In producing t-shirts as your LCVP enterprise, what factors would you take into account in deciding on **each** element of your marketing mix (4Ps)?

(c) In your LCVP activity/enterprise:
 (i) Identify one problem you encountered and explain how it was dealt with.
 (ii) What, in your opinion, were the main successes of the enterprise?
 (iii) Name two other Leaving Certificate subjects that helped you in completing your activity/enterprise, and give a reason for each choice.

(d) Describe three benefits of taking an active part in an LCVP activity or enterprise.

(e) Petra Kovak was always interested in woodwork. However, for a number of years she worked for a local garden centre. With the help of the local enterprise board she carried out market research on the landscape gardening industry and her research showed that a potential market existed in the area of custom-made garden furniture. With a loan from a bank, as well as a small amount of savings, she set up a small production enterprise to manufacture custom-built garden furniture. She now employs twelve people organised into four teams, each team specialising in different aspects of the business – garden sheds, garden tables/benches, ancillary furniture and delivery/installation. All the furniture is made specially to order for each customer.

(i) Identify two skills and two qualities that Petra needed when setting up her business.

(ii) Explain three benefits of working in teams.

(iii) Describe briefly how a local enterprise board can assist an entrepreneur when setting up a business.

(iv) Complete a SWOT analysis of Petra's business. Give at least one point under each heading.

(v) Give two advantages of having a business plan in place. Name four headings that would be contained in such a plan.

(f) Mike and Tina own a business, Milestone Ltd, which makes sportswear for children. The business operates in a small town and currently employs twelve people. Because of sport in schools, and local communities, Mike and Tina think that the business can be very successful. However, they are aware that they have to update their products in order to stay in business.

(i) Describe, briefly, three ways that Mike and Tina can find out what their customers want.

(ii) Explain the term 'marketing mix' (4Ps), with particular reference to Milestone Ltd.

(iii) Identify two other potential markets for Milestone Ltd.

(iv) Outline three steps that Milestone Ltd would need to complete in order to expand the business.

(v) Milestone Ltd has twelve employees. List two legal responsibilities the company has towards its employees.

(g) Your school has decided to apply for a 'Green Flag'. The LCVP class has been asked to draw up a plan of action to achieve the 'Green Flag'. A committee is formed and a chairperson elected.

(i) List and describe two skills and two qualities that a good leader should possess.

(ii) Set out, under four appropriate headings, a plan to achieve the 'Green Flag'.

(iii) Outline two ways that a local enterprise could assist the committee when undertaking this project.

(iv) Identify three different types of resources needed by the committee, and give one reason why each resource is important.

(h) (a) Success is very important for any business/enterprise.
    (i) State **three** ways success can be measured.
    (ii) Outline **two** ways a manager/owner of a business can ensure that the targets of the business are met.

(b) Explain the term 'Marketing Mix'. Give one example to illustrate your answer.

(c) Identify a product/service you might wish to promote. Outline an advertising campaign that you might put in place to promote this product/service.

(d) Why would it be important to evaluate the campaign? Explain how you could carry out an evaluation of the advertising campaign.

(2003 LCVP Examination)

(i) Your local area community association has asked for the help of your class. They want to improve the local facilities for young people and they have asked you to carry out research for them in your school.

(a) Why is research important?

(b) Draw up the questionnaire you would use to carry out the research in your school.

(c) What would you need to consider/plan for to ensure the survey was successful?

(d) What areas should be examined in evaluating the process?

(2004 LCVP Examination)

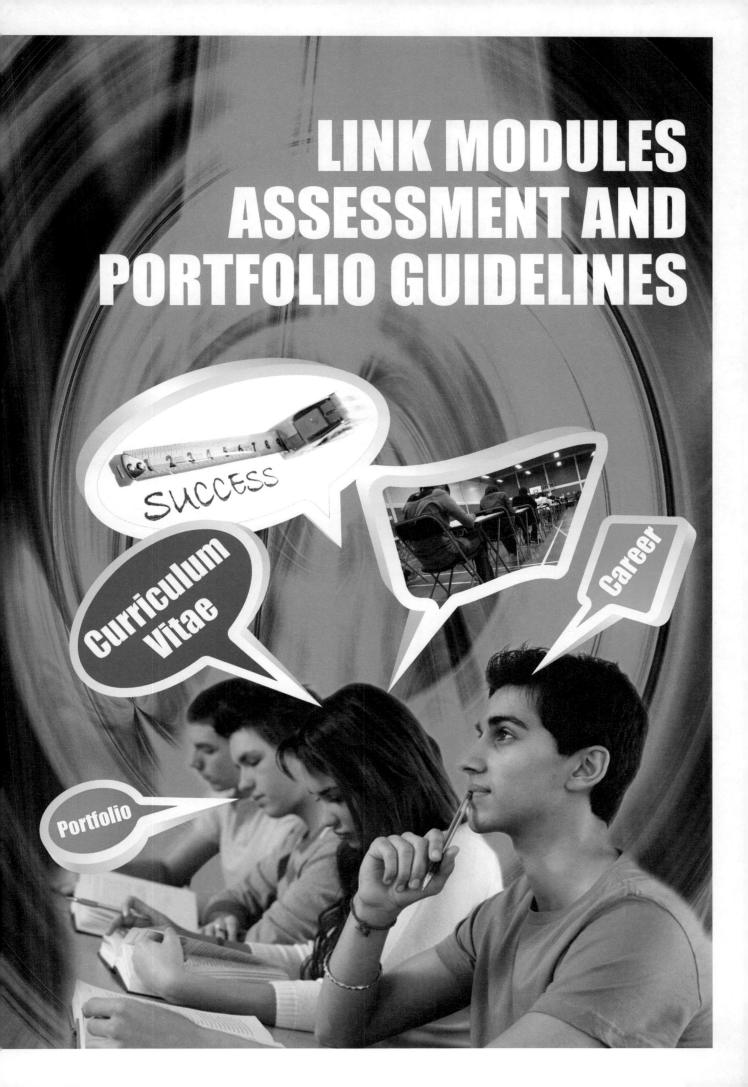

LCVP Portfolio Guidelines

Leaving Certificate Vocational Programme (LCVP)

The LCVP is currently assessed as follows:

Portfolio (of coursework)	**60%** of marks (240 marks)
Examination	**40%** of marks (160 marks)

The following are the current layout and guidelines for these two elements of the programme.

Examination

The LCVP examination currently takes place in May of the Leaving Certificate Year and is 2.5 hours long. The examination is divided into **three sections**:

Section	Description	Marks
Section A – Audio Visual	This section is of 30 minutes duration. The video will be shown a total of three times, and there are usually eight questions to be answered.	30 marks
Section B – Case Study	This is usually an account of a personal, community or business enterprise, or a local area. The Case Study is sent to each student approximately one month prior to the examination. There are usually three questions based on the Case Study.	30 marks
Section C – General Questions	This consists of six questions based on the Link Modules syllabus and the activities undertaken by the students over the two-year programme. The student must answer **four** questions.	100 marks

Portfolio

The LCVP portfolio will consist of **six** written items that are submitted for assessment. The portfolio consists of the following.

Core Items (Compulsory)
* Curriculum Vitae.
* Career Investigation.
* Summary Report.
* Enterprise/Action Plan.

Optional Items (Any 2)
* Work Experience Diary.
* Enterprise Report.
* Report on 'My Own Place'.
* Recorded Interview.

Core Items

Curriculum Vitae (CV)

The curriculum vitae (CV) should be a word-processed document up to **two A4 pages** in length. The CV should include at least four personal details, including the signature, and should be dated. It should also include 'Skills & Qualities', 'Educational Details', 'Work Experience', 'Achievements, Interests & Hobbies' and 'Referees' (including the referee's title, position and telephone number). See Chapter 2 for more details and a recommended layout. The CV is currently worth **25 marks**.

Career Investigation

The career investigation can be presented as a word-processed document of **300–600 words** in length, or as a **3–5 minute** interview on cassette tape (audio). The career investigation consists of the following.

* Title of career.
* Brief description of the career (including typical duties).
* At **least** two skills and two qualities needed for this career.
* Qualification and training requirements – **two** separate pathways must be shown.
* Reference to an out-of-class learning experience.
* Evaluation of the career with reference to your chosen subjects, interests and aptitudes.
* Evaluation of both the chosen career and of undertaking the career investigation.

See Chapter 3 for further details and a layout option. This item is worth **40 marks**. (Note: when undertaking the audiotape interview, it is very important that all of the above headings are included.)

Summary Report

The summary report should be a word-processed document of **300–600 words** in length. It can be written on any number of LCVP activities, including a visitor to the classroom, a visit out, an aspect of a 'My Own Place' investigation, an investigation of a voluntary organisation etc. The summary report should include the following.

* The title of the report.
* The name of the author.
* Terms of reference/aims of the activity.
* Introduction.
* Findings/activity.
* Conclusions and recommendations.

Note: no TWO portfolio items can be on the same activity – excluding the enterprise or action plan and the formal report on the activity afterwards.

Further information concerning the summary report can be found in Chapter 1. The summary report is worth **40 marks**.

Enterprise/Action Plan

The enterprise/action plan should be a word-processed document of **300–600 words** in length. The plan can be for an enterprise activity about to be undertaken by a student or a group, or be for an action (activity) that a student/group intends to undertake. The plan can be prepared for a mini-enterprise, a local area investigation, an activity to acquire a new skill, organising work experience/work shadowing, a visit out etc.

The plan should be in the **future tense**. However, you **must** show that you have already undertaken some research, and analysis thereof, as part of the initial investigation prior to completing the plan. Therefore, these parts of the plan – notably 'Research Methods' – should contain some details in the past tense.

Where group work is involved, it is very important to highlight your own individual contribution to the enterprise/action. One suggestion is the inclusion of a heading 'My Role' as part of the plan. You must also have one individual **personal objective** as part of the enterprise/action objectives.

The plan should include the following.
* **The title** – including 'A plan for …'.
* **Objectives** – two or three objectives, including one personal objective when it is a group activity.
* **Research methods** – should clearly indicate research already undertaken.
* **Analysis of research** – show the outcome of the research and how it will affect the plan.
* **Actions** – the steps to be undertaken to complete the enterprise/activity, in order of date.
* **My role** – if it is a group activity.
* **Schedule of time** – include finishing date, duration, time allocated to different parts of the activity etc. The schedule of time can be combined with the actions.
* **Resources and costs** – include the estimated cost of materials/expenses.
* **Evaluation methods** – how will you evaluate whether **each** of the objectives is achieved?

For further information, refer to Chapter 8. The enterprise/action plan is currently worth **35 marks**.

Optional Items (Choose Any 2)

Diary of Work Experience

The work experience diary can be presented either word-processed or hand-written, and should be **1,000–1,500 words** in length. The diary should be in chronological order. In the case of work experience, it should be a record of the student's experiences, observations, insights and evaluation of the experience. In the case of work shadowing, it should be a record of the student's in-school and out-of-school preparations, experiences, observations and evaluation of the work shadowing.

A possible layout for the diary is as follows.

* **Page 1** – name and description of the placement/work shadowing (include typical duties). Also give reasons for choosing the placement (e.g. career choice, experience/skills to be acquired, Leaving Certificate subjects taken etc.).

* **Pages 2–6** – one page per day is recommended, outlining duties, observations and experiences. There should be some analysis of personal performance in different situations. (There should be at least three dated entries.)
* **Page 7** – evaluation, with reference to:
  - the impact on study and career aspirations (hopes);
  - the relevance of skills/knowledge acquired or developed; and
  - how what has been learned can be applied to home/school/community.
* Up to two appendices may be included.

For more detailed information on the diary, see Chapter 4. The diary is currently worth **50 marks**.

Formal Report

The formal report should be a word-processed document **1,000–1,500 words** in length (not including the title page, table of contents or appendices). This is a report (in the past tense) on the activity that the student undertook as part of the LCVP.

The formal report should contain the following.

* **Title page** – including the title, author's name, who the report is for and the completion date.
* **Table of contents** – list of headings in order, with page numbers.
* **Terms of reference/aims of activity** – why the report was written and the objectives that it was hoped to achieve.
* **Summary** – a brief account of the enterprise, including the main conclusions and recommendations.
* **Body of the report** – include headings such as planning, research undertaken, organising tasks, the activity itself. At least two relevant illustrations should be included to support the main findings, e.g. chart, diagram etc. Larger diagrams, maps, photographs etc. can also be included in the appendices. If undertaking a group activity, a heading 'My Role' is recommended.
* **Conclusions** – should be based directly on the information in the report.
* **Recommendations** – based on the conclusions, these would include suggestions for future action.
* **Evaluation** – to what extent were the objectives achieved? How did the group/team perform? Were personal objectives achieved?
* **Appendices** – maximum of two items.

For more detailed information, see Chapter 8. This is currently worth **50 marks**.

Report on 'My Own Place'

This report should be a word-processed document **1,000–1,500 words** in length (not including the title page, table of contents or appendices). This is a report (in the past tense) on an investigation of 'My Own Place', and the issues raised, that the students undertook as part of the LCVP. For more detailed information see Chapter 1, and for a possible layout see **'My Portfolio'** on page 129.

As part of the report on 'My Own Place', the student must do the following.

* Identify and describe the local area.
* Define the aims and objectives.
* Outline the research methods.
* Describe an out-of-school activity as part of the investigation.
* Analyse the information gathered.
* Identify at least one important relevant local issue.
* Use maps, tables etc. as appropriate to support findings.
* Describe and evaluate their personal contribution.
* Reach conclusions and make recommendations relevant to the investigation.

The report on 'My Own Place' should contain the following.

* **Title page** – including title, author's name, who the report is for, and the completion date of the investigation.
* **Table of contents** – list of headings in order, with page numbers.
* **Introduction** – a brief description of the local area under investigation and the scope of the investigation.
* **Aims and objectives** – what they set out to investigate and the objectives it was hoped to achieve. Can include group and personal objectives.
* **Research methods** – the methods of collecting information etc.
* **Out-of-school activity** – date of activity, what took place, type of information gathered.
* **Findings** – this is the body of the report where the main findings of the investigation are described and analysed in a logical sequence. The student must identify and analyse an issue relevant to the local area, e.g. an issue identified as one of the objectives of the investigation (e.g. litter, child-care facilities) or an issue that has arisen as a result of the investigation (e.g. state of neglect of a local historical feature). This issue could be raised as a sub-heading. Small illustrations (maps, tables etc.) can be included here. Larger illustrations should be included in the appendices. It is also important to link the investigation and/or the findings to at least two other Leaving Certificate subjects.
* **Personal contribution** – this should be included as a heading, although the student should also highlight their personal role elsewhere, e.g. personal objective, evaluation of personal contribution.
* **Conclusions** – should be based on the information in the report and refer back to the objectives.
* **Recommendations** – based on the conclusions, these would include appropriate suggestions for future action.

* **Evaluation** – to what extent were the objectives achieved? How did the group/team perform? Evaluation of personal performance?
* **Appendices** – maximum of two items.

The report on 'My Own Place' is currently worth **50 marks**.

Recorded Interview/Presentation

This is a video recording (VHS or DVD) of the student being interviewed or making a presentation on some aspect of the Link Modules learning outcomes.

The content of the recorded interview/presentation cannot repeat content already covered by another portfolio item, e.g. summary report or work experience diary. A brief reference to an activity already covered by another portfolio item can be made during the recorded interview, but should not exceed 25% of the content/questions. (Note: the candidate's examination number must be identifiable.) The recorded interview/presentation should not exceed **5 minutes** duration.

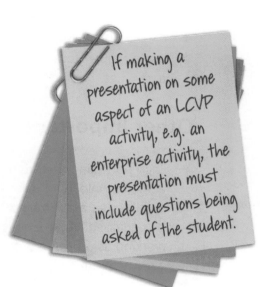

If making a presentation on some aspect of an LCVP activity, e.g. an enterprise activity, the presentation must include questions being asked of the student.

Recorded interviews/presentations can include the following.
* An interview/presentation on Link Module activities such as 'My Own Place' investigation, enterprise activity etc.
* A simulated job interview.

When undertaking a recorded interview/presentation, the student should take note of the following important details.
* Ensure that their appearance is neat and that they are dressed appropriately.
* Use a variety of tone, gesture etc.
* Make eye contact with the interviewer.
* Speak clearly and confidently.
* Express opinions and ideas clearly and knowledgeably.
* Express ideas/opinions/facts in a logical sequence.
* Avoid inappropriate language, reading from notes, distracting gestures etc.
* Make reference to skills/knowledge/experience gained.
* Highlight the benefits of the activity.

It is very important for the interviewer to plan the questions carefully so as to provide structure to the interview and proceed in a logical sequence. The interviewer should ask open questions and encourage the interviewee to express opinions and ideas.

The recorded interview/presentation is currently worth **50 marks**.

Overall Portfolio Format

The following guidelines should also be observed.

* The portfolio should have a cover page/contents page with the candidate's examination number and a list of the items contained in the portfolio for assessment.
* Should be presented on A4 pages in a soft covered folder, e.g. a binder. Do **not** place individual pages in plastic pockets.
* Margins of 2.5–3.75 cm are recommended.
* Clearly title **each** item in the portfolio.
* Use a regular font size (e.g. 12-point) and avoid clip-art, borders or using a variety of font types.

Other Important Issues Relevant to the Portfolio

* Each portfolio **must** be the student's own work. Copying information, other student's work, downloading directly from the Internet etc., is not acceptable and will be heavily penalised at assessment. (The student who allowed his/her work to be copied may also be penalised as the examiner will be unable to distinguish between them.) When working as part of a group, each student must submit his/her own **individual** plan, and elsewhere must highlight his/her individual contribution to the activity.
* The inclusion of non-LCVP material in the portfolio will result in marks not being awarded, e.g. diary of a school trip.
* Work undertaken as part of another programme, such as the Transition Year, is not acceptable.
* A candidate doing the LCVP who later repeats his/her Leaving Certificate will not be allowed to resubmit his/her portfolio. He/she will be allowed to re-sit the written examination, and the marks from the previous year's portfolio will be carried forward. The portfolio is the culmination of a two-year programme.
* No two items in the portfolio can cover the same activity, with the exception of the enterprise plan ('before') and the enterprise report ('after'), or an action plan ('before') followed by a report/interview ('after'). However, the plan **cannot** be reproduced as part of the report.

My Portfolio

'P.E.E.R' Pressure when undertaking activities:

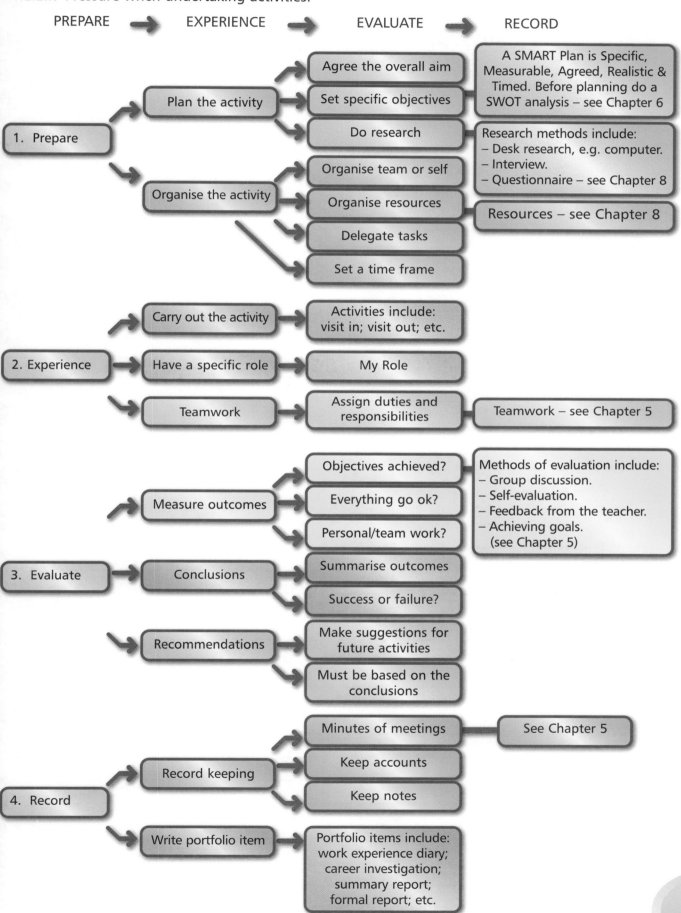

PREPARE → EXPERIENCE → EVALUATE → RECORD

1. Prepare

Plan the activity
- Agree the overall aim
- Set specific objectives
- Do research

A SMART Plan is Specific, Measurable, Agreed, Realistic & Timed. Before planning do a SWOT analysis – see Chapter 6

Research methods include:
– Desk research, e.g. computer.
– Interview.
– Questionnaire – see Chapter 8

Organise the activity
- Organise team or self
- Organise resources
- Delegate tasks
- Set a time frame

Resources – see Chapter 8

2. Experience

Carry out the activity
- Activities include: visit in; visit out; etc.

Have a specific role
- My Role

Teamwork
- Assign duties and responsibilities

Teamwork – see Chapter 5

3. Evaluate

Measure outcomes
- Objectives achieved?
- Everything go ok?
- Personal/team work?

Methods of evaluation include:
– Group discussion.
– Self-evaluation.
– Feedback from the teacher.
– Achieving goals.
  (see Chapter 5)

Conclusions
- Summarise outcomes
- Success or failure?

Recommendations
- Make suggestions for future activities
- Must be based on the conclusions

4. Record

Record keeping
- Minutes of meetings
- Keep accounts
- Keep notes

See Chapter 5

Write portfolio item
- Portfolio items include: work experience diary; career investigation; summary report; formal report; etc.

Summary Report – Core Portfolio

SUMMARY REPORT on _____

For the attention of: _____

_____

Prepared by: _____

Terms of Reference:

To write a report on the LCVP activity ... _____

_____

_____

The aims of the activity are:

-
-
-

Introduction:

_____

_____

_____

_____

Findings:

_____

_____

_____

_____

_____

_____

_____

_____

_____

_____

_____

_____

_____

_____

_____

Terms of Reference
Or
Aims of the activity.

Aims should include one personal aim.

Conclusion:

Recommendations:

NOTES:

Curriculum Vitae (CV) – Core Portfolio

CURRICULUM VITAE

PERSONAL DETAILS

Surname: _____

First Name: _____

Address: _____

_____

Phone No.: (_____) _____ e-mail: _____

EDUCATIONAL DETAILS

Primary School: _____

[_____ to _____] _____

Secondary School: _____

[_____ to _____] _____

Junior Certificate [20_____]

Subjects	Level	Grade

Leaving Certificate [20_____]

Subjects	Level	Grade

Link Modules must appear here.

WORK EXPERIENCE

Dates   Name of Organisation   Position/Role

_____   _____   _____

_____

_____

_____   _____   _____

_____

_____

INTERESTS & HOBBIES

- _____
- _____
- _____
- _____

ACHIEVEMENTS

- _____
- _____
- _____

SKILLS & QUALITIES

- _____
- _____
- _____
- _____

> Skills & Qualities can also be given as a short statement.

REFEREES

_____   _____

_____   _____

_____   _____

_____   _____

Tel. no. (___)_____   Tel. no. (___)_____

> Name, incl. title.
> Job title.
> Address.
> Phone no.

Signed: _____   Date: _____

Career Investigation – Core Portfolio

CAREER INVESTIGATION of _____

Prepared by: _____

Description of Career: _____
_____
_____
_____
_____
_____

Type of work and duties of the career.

Qualifications and Training required:

Pathway 1

Name: _____

Location: _____

Entry Requirements: _____
_____
_____

Points [20___]: _____

Description of Course:
_____
_____
_____
_____
_____
_____
_____
_____
_____

Qualification: _____

Pathway 2

Name: _____

Location: _____

Entry Requirements: _____
_____
_____

Points [20___]: _____

Description of Course:
_____
_____
_____
_____
_____
_____
_____
_____
_____

Qualification: _____

If there is only one pathway, then you must give a different career path.

Relevant Skills and Qualities:

- _____
- _____
- _____
- _____
- _____

Skills & Qualities relevant to the chosen career. Give 2–3 skills & 2–3 qualities.

Out of Class Learning Experience: _____

_____
_____
_____
_____
_____
_____
_____
_____
_____

Give dates, name of event, interview details etc.

Evaluation of Career in light of personal aptitudes, interests and choice of Leaving Certificate subjects:

_____
_____
_____
_____
_____
_____
_____
_____
_____
_____

Deal with all three aspects.

Evaluation of Career Investigation:

Career – _____

_____
_____
_____
_____
_____

Investigation – _____

_____
_____
_____
_____
_____
_____

Signed: _____   Date: _____

135

Enterprise Plan/Action Plan – Core Portfolio

PLAN OF _____

Team Members:
- _____
- _____
- _____

- _____
- _____

Aim: _____
_____

Objectives:

1. _____
_____

2. _____
_____

3. _____
_____

Research Methods:

1. _____
_____

2. _____
_____

3. _____
_____

Analysis of Research:

1. _____
_____
_____
_____

2. _____
_____
_____
_____

3. _____
_____
_____
_____

No specific number of team members.

The overall purpose.

At least two to three objectives. One objective should be personal.

Use at least two research methods. You must refer to some research which will be done.

Outline the information obtained, and to be obtained, and how it will influence the plan.

My Role:

_____

_____

Identify your specific role.

Actions:

_____

_____

_____

_____

_____

_____

_____

Plan of action to be followed, in chronological order.

Schedule of Time:

_____   _____

_____   _____

_____   _____

_____   _____

The schedule of time can be combined with the actions.

Resources and Costs:

Estimated Income – _____

Estimated Costs –

_____ = €_____

_____ = €_____

_____ = €_____

_____ = €_____

Total Costs   €_____

Surplus/Deficit   €_____

| Details of Income: |
| Details of Costs: |

Projected income (if any) and expenses should be itemised.

Evaluation Methods:

_____

_____

_____

_____

_____

_____

_____

Measures you will use to evaluate whether the objectives will be reached – incl. the personal objective.

All of page 2 of the plan **must be** in the future tense.

Diary – Optional Portfolio

WORK EXPERIENCE DIARY

Name of Workplace: _____

Description of Workplace: _____

_____

_____

_____

_____

_____

_____

Reason(s) for choosing this placement: _____

_____

_____

_____

_____

_____

Dates: _____

Summary of Duties: _____

_____

_____

_____

_____

_____

_____

_____

_____

_____

_____

_____

_____

_____

The reasons should reflect points such as career choice, subjects, interests, experience to be gained.

STUDENT WORK DIARY

Day: 1 Date: _____ Name of Supervisor: _____

What I did at work today: _____

| Minimum of three days. |

_____
_____
_____
_____
_____
_____

What new information I learned today: _____

_____
_____
_____
_____
_____

The main problems I experienced today: _____

_____
_____
_____

What I found most interesting: _____

_____
_____
_____

How I related with others: _____

_____
_____
_____

Evaluation of today: _____

_____
_____
_____
_____
_____
_____
_____
_____
_____

STUDENT WORK DIARY

Day: 2 Date: _____ Name of Supervisor: _____

What I did at work today: _____
_____
_____
_____
_____
_____

What new information I learned today: _____
_____
_____
_____

The main problems I experienced today: _____
_____
_____
_____

What I found most interesting: _____
_____
_____
_____

How I related with others: _____
_____
_____
_____

Evaluation of today: _____
_____
_____
_____
_____
_____
_____
_____

STUDENT WORK DIARY

Day: 3 Date: _____ Name of Supervisor: _____

What I did at work today: _____

_____

_____

_____

_____

_____

_____

What new information I learned today: _____

_____

_____

_____

_____

The main problems I experienced today: _____

_____

_____

_____

What I found most interesting: _____

_____

_____

_____

How I related with others: _____

_____

_____

_____

Evaluation of today: _____

_____

_____

_____

_____

_____

_____

_____

STUDENT WORK DIARY

Day: 4 Date: _____ Name of Supervisor: _____

What I did at work today: _____

_____

_____

_____

_____

_____

What new information I learned today: _____

_____

_____

_____

The main problems I experienced today: _____

_____

_____

_____

What I found most interesting: _____

_____

_____

_____

How I related with others: _____

_____

_____

_____

Evaluation of today: _____

_____

_____

_____

_____

_____

_____

_____

STUDENT WORK DIARY

Day: 5 Date: _____ Name of Supervisor: _____

What I did at work today: _____

_____

_____

_____

_____

_____

_____

What new information I learned today: _____

_____

_____

_____

_____

The main problems I experienced today: _____

_____

_____

_____

What I found most interesting: _____

_____

_____

_____

How I related with others: _____

_____

_____

_____

Evaluation of today: _____

_____

_____

_____

_____

_____

_____

_____

EVALUATION

Evaluate placement with regard to further study and career aspirations:

_____
_____
_____
_____
_____
_____
_____
_____
_____
_____

Skills/Experiences acquired or improved: _____

_____
_____
_____
_____
_____
_____

Evaluate how what has been learnt can be applied in the home, school, and community:

_____
_____
_____
_____
_____
_____
_____
_____
_____
_____
_____
_____
_____
_____

Make sure that you write a sentence about each of the three areas.

Two appendices can also be attached, e.g. employer's report.

Formal Report – Optional Portfolio

_____ REPORT

A Report on: _____

_____

Prepared by: _____

For the attention of: _____

Date: _____

TABLE OF CONTENTS

146

Summary:

_____
_____
_____
_____
_____
_____
_____
_____
_____
_____
_____
_____

A brief account of the activity, and the main conclusions and recommendations.

Terms of Reference:

_____
_____
_____
_____

Instructions given to the report writer.

Aims & Objectives:

_____
_____
_____
_____
- _____
- _____
- _____
- _____

State the overall aim, as well as specific objectives. At least one objective must be personal.
Hint: look back at the plan.

Introduction:

_____
_____
_____
_____
_____
_____
_____
_____

Some background information, e.g. how the activity came about.

Details of planning and the actions agreed.

Planning:

Give details of all research undertaken, and the results.

Research:

Marketing strategy – could refer to the 4Ps (Product, Price, Place and Promotion).

Marketing:

Organising the Event:

Delegation of tasks? Resources needed? Etc.

Actual Event:

Give a detailed account of the activity, in logical sequence. Should include at least two illustrations, e.g. table, chart.

Outline your specific role.

My Role:

Conclusions:

Recommendations:

The conclusions **must** be based on the body of the report and the stated objectives, e.g. were the targets reached?

Recommendations must be based on the conclusions, and make suggestions for future activities.

Evaluation:

Evaluate:
1. The activity.
2. Team work.
3. Personal performance.

Appendices
Can include up to two appendices e.g. tables, charts, photos.

Page 7

See page 182 for Appendix layout

151

My Own Place Report – Optional Portfolio

_____ REPORT

A Report on: _____

_____

Prepared by: _____

For the attention of: _____

Date: _____

TABLE OF CONTENTS

153

A brief description of your local area, and what aspect is under investigation. (could include map)
– See Chapter 1. Local area could be:
– housing estate
– village/town
– area around school.

Introduction:

_____
_____
_____
_____
_____
_____
_____
_____
_____
_____
_____
_____
_____

Instructions given to the report writer.

Terms of Reference:

_____
_____
_____

State the overall aim, as well as specific objectives. At least one objective should be personal.

Aims & Objectives:

_____
_____
_____

- _____
- _____
- _____
- _____

Details of planning, the actions agreed, and the scope of the investigation.

Planning:

_____
_____
_____
_____
_____
_____
_____
_____

Page 3

Research:

> Details of the research methods undertaken, e.g. interviews, observation, questionnaires etc.

Out of School Activity:

> Describe the activity, the date, the findings, the outcome etc. For example, field research involving the students investigating a local issue, e.g. tourist facilities, traffic etc.

Identify and analyse an issue relevant to the local area.
For example:
- A lack of sports facilities.
- Litter.
- Unemployment.
- Vandalism.
- Lack of funding for voluntary group.

You could refer to this issue in your objectives.

Summary of findings in a logical sequence. Include maps, tables etc.

Local Issue:

Findings:

My Role:

Conclusions:

Outline your specific role in the investigation.

Students must link the activity to at least two Leaving Certificate subjects.

157

The conclusions **must** be based on the findings of the report and refer back to the stated objectives.

Recommendations must be based on the conclusions, and make suggestions for:
1. Future investigations.
2. Local issues.

Recommendations:

Evaluate:
1. The investigation.
2. Team work.
3. Personal performance.

Evaluation:

Appendices
Can include up to two appendices e.g. tables, charts, photos.

Recorded Interview/Presentation – Optional Portfolio

Question 1:

Possible Answer (points):

- _____
- _____
- _____

- _____
- _____
- _____

Question 2:

Possible Answer (points):

- _____
- _____
- _____

- _____
- _____
- _____

Question 3:

Possible Answer (points):

- _____
- _____
- _____

- _____
- _____
- _____

Question 4:

Possible Answer (points):

- _____
- _____
- _____

- _____
- _____
- _____

Question 5:

Possible Answer (points):

- _____
- _____
- _____

- _____
- _____
- _____

Question 6:

Possible Answer (points):

- _____
- _____
- _____

- _____
- _____
- _____

Question 7:

Possible Answer (points):

- _____
- _____
- _____

- _____
- _____
- _____

Question 8:

Possible Answer (points):

- _____
- _____
- _____

- _____
- _____
- _____

NOTES:

LCVP Portfolio – Recommended Marking Scheme

Core Items – Compulsory

Curriculum Vitae	Marks
Word processing	1–2
Presentation/layout (conventional order)	1–3
Personal details (any four items including signature)	0–4
Skills and qualities	0–2
Educational qualifications	0–3
Work experience	0–3
Achievements/interests/hobbies	0–5
Referees	0–3
Total	**25**

Enterprise/Action Plan	
Presentation and layout	0–3
Title/purpose	0–2
Objectives (at least two needed)	0–4
Research methods	0–2
Analysis of research	0–6
Action steps	0–6
Schedule of time/costs	0–6
Evaluation methods	0–6
Total	**35**

Career Investigation	
Title/word processing/use of headings (*or audio tape*)	0–5
Description of duties involved in the career/area	0–3
Identification of skills and qualities needed	0–5
Identification of qualifications and training needed	0–5
What was learned by the research/activity about career and one-self	0–8
Description of two different pathways to the career	0–4
Evaluation: of the career	0–5
of undertaking the career investigation	0–5
Total	**40**

Summary Report	
Presentation layout	1–5
Title/name of activity	0–5
Author's name	0/5
Terms of reference of report/aims of the activity	0/3/5
Body of report – content (short sentences, summaries, appropriate language)	1–10
Body of report – clarity (headings, logical structure, flow, originality of thought)	1–5
Conclusions/recommendations	1–5
Total	**40**
TOTAL OF CORE ITEMS	**140**

Optional Items – Any Two	
Record/Log/Diary	**Marks**
Presentation/layout	0–5
Name and description of work experience placement	0–5
Reasons for choosing work experience placement	0–5
Content	
Factual day to day account of at least 3 days/entries as follows:	
Detailed personalised account	0–10
Candidate analysis of own performance in different situations	0–10
Expression and evaluation	
Evaluation of experience in the light of study and career aspirations	0–5
Evaluation of how what has been learnt can be applied to work in the home, school and the local community	0–10
Total	50
Report (Formal)	
Presentation/layout	0–4
Title/table of contents	0–2
Author's name or signature	0–2
Terms of reference of report/aims of activity	0–4
Summary of main points	0–4
Body of report (may include personal contribution)	
Account of activity	0–10
Use of appropriate depth, detail, organisation of information	0–8
Use of charts, tables, diagrams	0–4
Conclusions/recommendations	0–6
Evaluation	0–6
Total	50
My Own Place – Report	
Presentation/layout	0–4
Title/table of contents	0–2
Description of local area/what is under investigation	0–5
Aims/objectives	0–5
Research methods	0–5
Body of report – description and analysis of key aspects	0–6
– use of logical sequence/headings/illustrations	0–5
– analysis of issue/suggestions for improvements	0–6
Conclusions and recommendations	0–6
Evaluation	0–6
Total	50
Recorded Interview/Presentation	
Presentation (neat in the context of the interview/presentation)	0–4
Variety of tone, gesture, diction, eye contact	0–4
Ability to communicate message clearly, engage audience, elaborate on points/questions, logical sequence of thought	0–36
Pass (18–23) – basic communication skills	
Merit (24–27) – ability to express ideas and opinions clearly and knowledge of topic	
Distinction (28–36) – knowledge and ability to communicate ideas and own opinions clearly and in logical sequence	
Information (content)	0–6
Total	50
TOTAL OF OPTIONAL ITEMS	**100**

(Source: State Examinations Commission)

LCVP
EXAMINATION PAPERS
2005–2009

Leaving Certificate Vocational Programme
Link Modules Examination 2005

Section A	Audio Visual	30 marks

Part 1

1. Name **two** enterprises Pádraig Ó Céidigh was involved in. (2 marks)
2. Give **two** difficulties he faced when setting up Aer Arann. (2 marks)
3. How has the enterprise grown in the past 10 years? Give **two** ways. (2 marks)

Part 2

4. Give **two** reasons why Micheál's job is important for the company. (4 marks)
5. Micheál was required to move to Dublin on taking up his position.
   Why was this necessary and what changes to his lifestyle were involved? (4 marks)
6. Describe **two** challenges Micheál identifies that face Aer Arann now. (4 marks)

Part 3

7. How would you describe **and** measure the impact of Aer Arann on
   development in the western seaboard of Ireland over the past 10 years? (6 marks)
8. Set out below a SWOT analysis for Aer Arann with an explanation for
   each point made. (6 marks)

Section B	Case Study	30 marks

Community Development

Ballytra is situated 80 kilometres from the nearest city and 20 kilometres from four other large towns. The town has an attractive river running through it with a large oak forest to the west of the town. There is one primary school, a community college and a community training centre located in the town. There is one old hotel with sixteen rooms which is in need of refurbishment. A 19th century country house, in need of repair, with a nine-hole golf course attached to it is situated 8 kilometres from the town.

Ballytra is home to a company called Choc O'Late Ltd. for the past eight years. This is a confectionery business owned by two brothers. It is situated on an industrial site just outside the town. This company has sixty-five employees. In 2002 the turnover was nine million euro but this has decreased to seven million euro in 2004 due to the lack of demand for confectionery products. Also, increased competition and increases in insurance and wage costs have affected the company. This has led to some employees losing their jobs and the company is now talking of downsizing their business further having conducted an audit of the company's finances.

Due to the job losses in Choc O'Late Ltd. and lack of continued new employment in the area, local people realised their children would not be in a position to settle down in the town in the future. This jolted them into action and the business community and local people were invited to a public meeting. Here, various ideas and proposals were discussed. Several enterprise ideas were put forward which could be developed in the area. The challenges of setting up new business ventures in the town are very significant especially with regard to necessary resources and expertise.

A community development committee was selected to oversee any development initiatives. The intention of the committee is to use a local resource audit to establish the community's resources and strengths and to try to negotiate the establishment of a Business Park with local authorities. Certain members of the committee are highly environmentally conscious and would like to see socially and environmentally responsible businesses set up in their town.

Answer all questions.
1. What facilities do teenagers require in, or near, their home town? (6 marks)
2. Choc O'Late Ltd. is considering downsizing its operations.
    What alternatives should be considered before this decision is taken? (12 marks)
3. The community development committee decides to draw up a document outlining the attractions of the town for potential enterprises.
    (a) Put, in order of priority, your list of advantages of Ballytra and briefly explain each.
    (b) What are the disadvantages of a Business Park in the area?
    (c) Draw up a list, in order of importance, of the qualities required by the committee in enterprises applying to locate in the proposed Business Park. (12 marks)

Section C General Questions 100 marks

Section C contains 6 questions of 25 marks each. You should answer any four questions.

1. **Career Investigation introduces students to skills of career research and planning.**
    (a) Name a career you have investigated. (1 mark)
    (b) Identify and analyse **three** aptitudes or skills that are required to follow this specific career. (6 marks)
    (c) Having identified a suitable career, describe **three** steps you now need to take to reach your career goal. (8 marks)
    (d) Evaluate in **three** ways the career investigation process. (10 marks)

2. Enterprise is essential for progress.
   (a) What is your understanding of enterprise? (2 marks)
   (b) Explain **one** example of enterprise in action in each of the following areas:
       (i) Household.
       (ii) School.
       (iii) Community. (6 marks)
   (c) Discuss **three** benefits entrepreneurs bring to society. (9 marks)
   (d) Describe **four** ways an entrepreneur could evaluate his/her success. (8 marks)

3. You have decided to raise funds for your school by holding a disco.
   (a) Draw up an agenda for a class meeting for this activity. (4 marks)
   (b) What are the advantages of having a business plan? (4 marks)
   (c) Describe a business plan for a school disco under **three** distinct headings. (9 marks)
   (d) How, in order of importance, would you evaluate this business plan? (8 marks)

4. A good idea is often the basis for a successful enterprise.
   (a) List **four** methods of 'idea generation'. (4 marks)
   (b) Explain the importance of **SWOT** analysis in providing opportunities
       for an enterprise. (5 marks)
   (c) List the **four** P's of the marketing mix and explain **one** of them. (10 marks)
   (d) Discuss **two** implications the Single European Market has for
       enterprises in Ireland. (6 marks)

5. All students have participated in work experience/shadowing and produced a
   diary/log.
   (a) Why is work experience/shadowing useful? (3 marks)
   (b) List and explain **four** personal goals you had in relation to work
       experience/shadowing you have undertaken. (8 marks)
   (c) (i) Identify **two** ways of finding work experience/shadowing.
       (ii) Outline **two** advantages for any one of the ways you have listed. (6 marks)
   (d) Summarise below the evaluation you submitted in your diary/log in
       your portfolio. (8 marks)

6. Your class visited a local community enterprise or voluntary organisation
   as part of LCVP.
   (a) Name an organisation you have visited and give a brief outline of the
       work/service it provides. (3 marks)
   (b) Outline **two** reasons why you would have undertaken the above visit. (6 marks)
   (c) Describe **four** essential steps you would take in preparing for this visit. (8 marks)
   (d) Write a letter to a friend in America describing what you have learned
       from this visit. (8 marks)

Leaving Certificate Vocational Programme Link Modules Examination 2006

Section A	Audio Visual	30 marks

Part 1

1. Why was the Society of St. Vincent de Paul formed? (1 mark)
2. What does Columba see as her role as National Secretary within the Society of St. Vincent de Paul? (2 marks)
3. What sources of income does the Society have? (3 marks)

Part 2

4. What is the work of the Society? (4 marks)
5. Describe Brendan's role in the Society. (4 marks)
6. What personal qualities does Brendan consider important for his role? (4 marks)

Part 3

7. How many people are working for the Society and describe a **relevant** trend. (6 marks)
8. Identify three **other** trends mentioned in the video and indicate the Society's plans for the next three years. (6 marks)

Section B	Case Study	30 marks

recruit2suit

John O'Reilly, after leaving college in 1995 with a Business degree, went to work in a large bank, working there for six years. He was quickly promoted to the Human Resources department where part of his job was to engage new staff for the bank. During this time John gained considerable experience of, and skills in, the recruitment area. He believed that the Irish economy was entering another boom period and this would encourage businesses to expand and increase their staff numbers. He decided to become his own boss and to set up his own recruitment agency. John felt he had a lot of fresh ideas and that he could make a success of this business.

Having completed extensive market research, John became more aware of the challenges facing him. He sought help from bodies promoting and developing enterprise. They offered support and advice in finance, management and, particularly, marketing. They recommended that summaries of these areas should be included in his 'business plan' as an aid to defining the proposed business and to gaining financial support. He spent considerable time preparing this document and it helped him secure a substantial loan from a bank.

John started his business in a local business park, initially employing four staff. He invested heavily in 'state of the art' Information and Communication Technology. Four years later, John is the owner of a very successful and profitable business. He now has leased offices in the same business park and employs twenty-two staff vetting applications and recommending suitable candidates to employers.

John suspects, however, that his business is too heavily dependent on recruitment and is investigating other opportunities for the security, survival and success of the firm in the longer term. This rethink has been further encouraged by a request from a multinational company for his firm to provide services for its large worldwide Research and Development facilities.

Answer all questions.

1. Describe the entrepreneurial qualities/characteristics displayed by John in this Case Study. (6 marks)
2. John prepared a business plan when looking for his first bank loan.
   (i) Why was completing market research important? (3 marks)
   (ii) Set out the marketing section of this plan using **three** relevant headings. (9 marks)
3. Describe what other opportunities John could explore. What are the implications of **each** of those for the business? (12 marks)

Section C	General Questions	100 marks

Section C contains 6 questions of 25 marks each. You should answer any four questions.

1.

POSITION AVAILABLE

For an **enterprising** young person to join the
Sales and Marketing team of a new telecommunication company.

Apply with a Curriculum Vitae to:
Personnel Manager,
O'Keeffe Enterprises,
Unit 2 Waterside Business Park,
New Ross, Co. Wexford.
Telephone: 053 123456. email: okeeffeent@irl.ie

*O'Keeffe Enterprises is an **equal opportunities** employer.*

Study the newspaper advertisement (left) and answer the following questions.

(a) Explain the underlined words: 'enterprising' **and** 'equal opportunities'. (4 marks)

(b) Outline **three** other methods by which job vacancies may be made known. (6 marks)

(c) Describe **three** ways you would prepare for a job interview. (6 marks)

(d) One of the interviewers asks: "Why should we offer you this position?" What would be your response? Justify your answers. (9 marks)

2. 'Teamwork is important in the modern workplace'.

(a) Outline an LCVP activity in which you participated in a team **and** indicate your role. (4 marks)

(b) Identify **three** benefits of teamwork in this activity. (6 marks)

(c) Describe what makes a person a good team member. (6 marks)

(d) Describe **three** ways a team can evaluate its group performance. (9 marks)

3. As part of your Leaving Certificate Vocational Programme you are required to undertake work placement/shadowing in light of your career aspirations.

(a) Name this career **and** identify **two** skills/qualities required to pursue it. (3 marks)

(b) Explain **three** benefits to you of having participated in work placement/shadowing. (6 marks)

(c) Outline how you planned for, **and** organised yourself, during this work placement/shadowing. (7 marks)

(d) Identify **and** explain **three** obligations an employer has regarding the health, safety and welfare of their employees at work. (9 marks)

4. Your Links Module Group has decided to organise a school '5 a side' soccer competition.

(a) Set out the agenda for the first meeting of the group. (5 marks)

(b) Prepare the minutes of that first meeting. (6 marks)

(c) Set out the section of your action plan which deals with the running of this activity. (8 marks)

(d) How would you evaluate the success of this activity? (6 marks)

5. 'Financial Planning is important for a successful enterprise'.

(a) (i) Name an enterprise activity you have participated in. (1 mark)

(ii) Outline **two** financial resources you used to support this enterprise activity. (4 marks)

(b) Explain the importance of financial planning for your enterprise. (6 marks)

(c) Outline **three** ways participation in this activity has been of benefit to you as a student. (6 marks)

(d) Describe **four** ways by which this enterprise could be evaluated. (8 marks)

169

6. 'Your class has decided to organise/plan a visit by an appropriate speaker from a local Community Organisation'.

   (a) List **four** objectives your class might have for this visit. (4 marks)

   (b) What steps should be taken to ensure that this visit is organised **and** run efficiently? (4 marks)

   (c) Describe **four** ways the local community benefits from this organisation. (8 marks)

   (d) Name **three** Leaving Certificate subjects, other than Link Modules, you are studying and indicate how **each** was useful in the organisation/ planning of **this** visit and how this activity helped you in each subject. (9 marks)

Leaving Certificate Vocational Programme
Link Modules Examination 2007

Section A	Audio Visual	30 marks

Part 1
1. Why was Radio na Life (RnL) established? (1 mark)
2. What are the distinctive audiences that RnL has? (2 marks)
3. What does RnL contribute to its community? (3 marks)

Part 2
4. What qualities are required by Feargal in his job? (4 marks)
5. What issues frustrate Feargal and why? (4 marks)
6. Describe the teamwork required in running RnL. (4 marks)

Part 3
7. What are the factors that RnL, as a community station, have to address? (6 marks)
8. What factors will affect the future development of RnL? (6 marks)

Section B	Case Study	30 marks

KeeParts Ltd
Michael O'Neill graduated from Cork University with a degree in Electronic Engineering. On leaving college he was recruited by a large multi-national firm to work as a Production Engineer based in their European headquarters in Paris. He was responsible for the production of components to be used in the manufacture of domestic appliances. During the ten years that Michael worked with the company he gained lots of experience and won the respect of many by his up to date knowledge and his enthusiastic approach.

While Michael was quite happy in his job, he always had a desire to work for himself, and to set up his own business. Having secured an attractive early retirement financial package he returned to Ireland two years ago and set up KeeParts Ltd. He leased a small commercial unit in a business park which is strategically located just 10 km from the nearest city.

Michael had built up a lot of contacts over the years and is currently manufacturing components under contract for a large European washing machine manufacturer.

He invested heavily in the firm through his savings and the financial package he received on leaving the multi-national. He was also delighted to receive assistance from a state agency.

Recently he was approached by two other companies to manufacture components under licence for them. Currently he employs ten people and he carries out all the management functions himself. He would be unable to expand his business from his present location and Michael is well aware of the demands that expanding the firm may bring.

Michael feels that he cannot delay making this decision as it is a chance that may not come his way again. He is well aware of the importance of supplying high quality components to as many customers as possible, in order to ensure the success of his business.

Answer all questions.

1. State and explain the advantages to Michael of setting up his own business. (6 marks)
2. (i) What assistance can state agencies offer entrepreneurs? (4 marks)
   (ii) Prepare a SWOT analysis for KeeParts Ltd. (8 marks)
3. Describe **four** possible implications of expansion for KeeParts Ltd. (12 marks)

Section C	General Questions	100 marks

Section C contains 6 questions of 25 marks each. You should answer any four questions.

1. Enterprise is important for successful organisations.
   (a) Name an entrepreneur in your own community. (2 marks)
   (b) Describe the enterprising characteristics of that person. (6 marks)
   (c) Describe **four** ways in which the success of an enterprise can be measured. (8 marks)
   (d) Contrast the role of an entrepreneur with that of a manager. (9 marks)

2. A visit out by your class to a business or organisation.
   (a) Distinguish between profit making and non-profit making organisations. (4 marks)
   (b) Name a business or organisation your class has visited as part of the Links Modules. (1 mark)
   (c) Describe **two** factors that contributed to the success/failure of the visit. (6 marks)
   (d) (i) Why is it important to evaluate your visit? (5 marks)
       (ii) Describe **three** methods that could be used to evaluate the visit out, with a reason for choosing each method. (9 marks)

3. Career Investigation is an important part of choosing a suitable career.
   (a) Name a career you have investigated as part of the Link Modules. (1 mark)
   (b) Identify **three** sources of information you used to investigate the career and outline how each source was relevant. (6 marks)
   (c) Describe **three** methods of evaluating the career investigation activity. (9 marks)
   (d) Describe **three** changes in Irish employment trends in recent years. (9 marks)

4. Voluntary enterprises make important contributions to the local community.
   (a) Name a voluntary organisation or community enterprise in your local area. (1 mark)
   (b) Write a detailed account of the above body under **four** relevant headings. (8 marks)
   (c) Identify and describe a community need not currently being met locally. (8 marks)
   (d) What suggestions would you make to address that need. (8 marks)

5. You are required to undertake appropriate work experience/shadowing as part of the Link Modules programme.
   (a) Outline **one** method of finding work experience/shadowing. (3 marks)
   (b) Explain **three** benefits of engaging in work experience/shadowing. (6 marks)
   (c) Describe how the 'school experience' can help in this activity. (6 marks)
   (d) (i) Outline **three** benefits of Health and Safety regulations in the workplace. (6 marks)
       (ii) Explain the obligations of an employee in relation to Health and Safety. (4 marks)

6. Planning is important for successful enterprises.
   (a) Why is a 'business plan' important for an enterprise? (2 marks)
   (b) Describe **three** challenges that a new enterprise might face. (6 marks)
   (c) In the case of an activity/enterprise in which you were involved in the course of the Link Modules, prepare a business plan using **four** appropriate headings. (8 marks)
   (d) Evaluate your participation in this activity/enterprise under **three** distinct headings. (9 marks)

Leaving Certificate Vocational Programme
Link Modules Examination 2008

Section A	Audio Visual	30 marks

Part 1

1. What services did Top Solutions offer when it was first set up? (1 mark)
2. How did Top Solutions develop the business services it offers? (2 marks)
3. What personal qualities did Mary require in her role as manager? (3 marks)

Part 2

4. What prompted Mary to consider a change in her work? (4 marks)
5. Explain the legal requirements that Mary, as an employer, complied with. (4 marks)
6. In what way does Mark consider he can contribute to Top Solutions success? (4 marks)

Part 3

7. What steps does Mary take to overcome the risks associated with being self-employed? (6 marks)
8. What are Top Solutions strengths? Give reasons why you have chosen each. (6 marks)

Section B	Case Study	30 marks

Community Development

Ballynure is a small rural town situated 50 kilometres from the nearest city and 30 kilometres from the nearest rail network. The railway station in Ballynure closed over thirty years ago and the only public transport available now is a very limited bus service. The old station house has been converted into a number of business units, which are now occupied by people involved in arts and crafts. Some of these enterprises operate on a seasonal basis only and overall Ballynure offers very little by way of large-scale job opportunities for its community.

The town is very picturesque and tranquil. The majority of the people are involved in either agriculture or tourism. Others commute to their employment in the nearest city. Tourism is very important to the town and many visitors come to fish in the nearby lakes. Ballynure has two primary schools and a community school. Most of the young people leave the area to go to college or to work and are unlikely to return because of the lack of employment opportunities.

Ballynure has one big employer that manufactures biscuits and confectionery. Competition and increasing costs are now beginning to impact on this business and the management of the firm are wondering whether to take on the competition by further investment or to downsize and settle for a smaller share of the market. The future is bleak for Ballynure and unless action is taken immediately the problems may escalate.

This situation has prompted some members of the community to be more proactive. Business people and interested parties have been invited to a public meeting to discuss and to address the issues facing the town. The development of an Industrial Park is one of the ideas being mentioned which would create opportunities in different sectors. However, any type of development must not be damaging to the environment or adversely affect the quality of life enjoyed by the current residents.

Answer all questions.

1. State and explain **three** problems facing the town of Ballynure? (6 marks)
2. (i) Describe the opportunities and/or challenges the Community Group might face.
   (ii) Describe the possible difficulties the Community Group might encounter whilst promoting enterprise. (12 marks)
3. Outline **four** negative implications for the people of Ballynure if the proposed Industrial Park goes ahead. (12 marks)

| Section C | General Questions | 100 marks |

Section C contains 6 questions of 25 marks each. You should answer any four questions.

1. **Enterprise is essential for progress.**
   (a) Explain what you understand by the term 'enterprise'. (2 marks)
   (b) List **four** methods a business enterprise could use to generate ideas. (4 marks)
   (c) Describe **two** examples of enterprise in action in each of the following areas:
      (i) Household.
      (ii) Local Community. (8 marks)
   (d) Consider your participation in the drawing up of an LCVP enterprise/action plan for a class activity.
      (i) Identify **one** Leaving Certificate subject that has helped you. State why.
      (ii) Outline in detail **three** ways your participation in the activity will benefit you in the future. (11 marks)

2. Planning is essential for a business to succeed.
   (a) Outline **three** reasons why it is important for a business to plan. (6 marks)
   (b) Name and explain **two** areas that would be included as part of the body of a Business Plan. Include why each is important. (4 marks)
   (c) Consider the location of an enterprise/organisation you are familiar with. Outline **three** reasons why it is located there. (6 marks)
   (d) Name a business enterprise with which you are familiar and carry out a SWOT analysis for that business. (9 marks)

3. Work placements offer students a valuable opportunity to experience the world of work.
   (a) List **three** reasons why work shadowing/work experience is useful to students. (3 marks)
   (b) Describe **four** difficulties that a student may experience during his/her work shadowing/work experience. (8 marks)
   (c) Identify and explain the obligations that employers have regarding the health, safety and welfare of their employees. (6 marks)
   (d) Write a formal letter to an employer in your area seeking work experience/work shadowing as part of your Link Modules programme. (8 marks)

4. Planning an event is an essential class activity to enhance learning.
   (a) As part of your LCVP enterprise module your class has decided to organise a careers exhibition. A class meeting has been called to begin the organising of the event. Draw up an agenda for this meeting. (7 marks)
   (b) Identify and explain **three** benefits of working as part of a team when undertaking the activity. (6 marks)
   (c) Why is it important to evaluate the activity? (3 marks)
   (d) Describe **three** ways that the organisation of the careers exhibition could be evaluated. Give reasons for choosing each. (9 marks)

5. An important role is played by community organisations/enterprises in society.
   (a) Explain why people get involved in community organisations. (3 marks)
   (b) Describe **three** benefits that voluntary organisations/community enterprises bring to local communities. (6 marks)
   (c) (i) Describe **two** ways in which commercial businesses may give support to a voluntary organisation/community enterprise.
   (ii) Explain, giving **one** reason, why commercial businesses might do this. (6 marks)
   (d) Write a short summary report of a **visit-in** or a **visit-out** that you participated in to a voluntary organisation/community enterprise. Use appropriate headings. (10 marks)

6. School and college is about training young people for the world of work.
   (a) Name **four** pieces of advice you would give to a friend when filling out
       a job application form. (4 marks)
   (b) Describe **three** non-financial benefits to be gained from the world
       of work. (6 marks)
   (c) Outline **three** ways in which the world of work differs from school work. (6 marks)
   (d) Give **three** characteristics that employers might look for in potential
       employees. Explain why you think employers consider each characteristic
       to be important. (9 marks)

Leaving Certificate Vocational Programme Link Modules Examination 2009

Section A — Audio Visual — 30 marks

Part 1

1. Name one stakeholder in a business. (1 mark)
2. What are the benefits of corporate social responsibility to businesses? (2 marks)
3. Explain two ways that a business can support voluntary or community projects. (4 marks)

Part 2

4. Explain **three** skills demonstrated by those who volunteer on the Niall Mellon Project. (3 marks)
5. Describe **two** of the benefits to the business of working with a local community. (4 marks)
6. How can a business's efforts at improving its reputation be seen outside the organisation? (4 marks)

Part 3

7. How is social obligation acted out by businesses? (6 marks)
8. Describe some of the ways that organisations can ensure that their community involvement is effective? (6 marks)

Section B — Case Study — 30 marks

Car Care

From a very young age Frank Carr had a keen interest in cars and engines. He helped his older brother when he was working on his car and spent most of his pocket money on car magazines and going to car rallies. When he completed his Leaving Certificate in 1999 he decided to take up an apprenticeship as a trainee mechanic with a local garage.

While serving his time Frank worked from home in the evening and on Saturdays doing repairs for friends and other contacts that he had built up over time. Frank was working every available minute and soon realised it would be impossible to keep working in the garage and also make time for the work he was undertaking on his own. After finishing his apprenticeship in 2003 he decided that when a suitable premises became available he would set up his own business and put all his efforts into running this business. His aim was to satisfy the needs of his existing customers as well as attracting new customers. That opportunity came in 2004 when Frank took a lease out on a premises and set up Car Care. He financed the business by using his own personal savings and negotiating a bank loan.

The premises was ideally located with plenty of space so Frank decided to offer a car-wash and valeting service together with the normal repairs and maintenance service. Frank was extremely dedicated to the business and was constantly thinking of finding new ways of increasing his customer base and of making more services available to them. The lease on the original premises expired in 2007 and Frank decided to move to a larger premises which would allow him further scope to expand. He could now offer a panel beating, crash repairs as well as a tyre and exhaust service in addition to what he was already offering. His idea was to create a "one stop shop" to maximise the opportunity while also making it convenient for a customer to have all the required services at one location.

This venture required a huge investment and Frank borrowed heavily in order to finance the necessary equipment, fittings, stock, and machinery. When negotiating loans with the bank the Manager has always been impressed by Frank's drive and ambition to succeed. Initially Car Care employed ten people but since moving to the new location the number of employees has increased to fifty. Frank is a firm believer in the importance of teamwork together with maintaining a high level of customer satisfaction.

In addition, Frank values the importance of information and communications technology, and as the business grows he sees it as a prerequisite for success to keep investing in that area. Car Care is now establishing itself as a market leader. It has built up a reputation for good quality services offered by a very capable workforce. Frank's energy, drive and commitment are essential to Car Care's continued success together with his willingness to take risks and finance expansion through borrowing and reinvesting.

Answer all questions.
1. Identify and explain the benefits that teamwork brings to Car Care.   (6 marks)
2. Information and communications technology (ICT) has an important role in business. Identify **four** aspects of ICT which Car Care might be using and describe how each would be used. Give an advantage and disadvantage of each.   (12 marks)
3. (i) What are the implications of an enlarged Single European Market for Car Care.
   (ii) Outline **four** areas of the business that Frank must continually focus on to ensure continued success.   (12 marks)

Section C	General Questions	100 marks

Section C contains 6 questions of 25 marks each. You should answer any four questions.

1. Understanding enterprise is a key element of the Leaving Certificate Vocational Programme.
    (a) List **two** qualities of an enterprising person. Give **one** reason why each quality is important. (4 marks)
    (b) Identify and explain **three** essential elements needed to successfully set up a business enterprise. (9 marks)
    (c) Outline **three** ways that the owner of a business can ensure that customer demands are satisfied. (6 marks)
    (d) Success is essential for the survival of a business enterprise. Describe **three** ways that success can be measured. (6 marks)

2. Work experience/shadowing and the preparation of a diary gives a valuable opportunity for students to experience and reflect on the world of work.
    (a) List **four** steps you took to secure a suitable placement for your work experience/shadowing. (4 marks)
    (b) List and explain **three** personal goals you had in relation to work experience/shadowing. (6 marks)
    (c) Describe the steps a person should undertake when preparing for a job interview. (6 marks)
    (d) (i) Why is it important to evaluate your work experience/shadowing?
        (ii) Outline the evaluation prepared by you as part of your diary/log. (9 marks)

3. As part of your Leaving Certificate Vocational Programme you are encouraged to become actively involved in setting up a mini company.
    (a) List **four** methods an enterprise uses to generate ideas. (4 marks)
    (b) Explain what you understand by the term market research. (5 marks)
    (c) List the **four** P's of the marketing mix and explain **one** of them. (7 marks)
    (d) Outline why it is important for a business to undertake market research. (9 marks)

4. An awareness of the areas in which we live and where we work is important.
    (a) Name **one** agency or business involved in each of the following.
        (i) Job creation. (ii) Financial services. (iii) Transport services. (3 marks)
    (b) Consider an agency/business you mentioned in part (a) and describe the significance of this agency/business to the area. (4 marks)
    (c) Prepare a questionnaire you would use to do an investigation of your local area. (10 marks)
    (d) What challenges might your local area face over the next five years? Suggest how these might be overcome. (8 marks)

5. Career investigation helps students to identify a career which links with their interests and aptitudes.
    (a) Name a career you have investigated. (1 mark)
    (b) List **three** qualities and **three** skills you have which makes this a suitable career for you. (6 marks)
    (c) Describe **three** methods of evaluating the career investigation activity. (9 marks)
    (d) What options are available to you if you become unemployed and you wish to return to work? Explain your answers. (9 marks)

6. Voluntary bodies/community enterprises play an important role in the areas in which they operate. A visiting speaker from a voluntary body/community enterprise has agreed to give a presentation to your class.
    (a) Name a voluntary body or a community enterprise that operates in your local area. (1 mark)
    (b) Identify and explain **three** differences between voluntary bodies/community enterprises and commercial business enterprises. (6 marks)
    (c) What steps should be taken to ensure that the visit-in is organised properly and run efficiently? (6 marks)
    (d) (i) Outline the issues that arise for this organisation.
        (ii) Explain **three** objectives that the class might have for organising the visit. (12 marks)

Sample Layout   NIALL MAHER

APPENDIX

Appendices
Can include up to
two appendices
e.g. tables, charts,
photos.

Examples:
Costs (pie chart) –

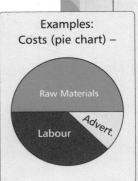

Raw Materials

Labour   Advert.

Table:

Incomes:

Expenditure:

Surplus/deficit

Other examples
include:
- Advertising poster
- Questionnaire
- Photograph
- Map
- Copy of letter sent
  or received